Ecocollapse Fiction and Cultures of Human Extinction

Environmental Cultures Series

Series Editors:
Greg Garrard, University of British Columbia, Canada
Richard Kerridge, Bath Spa University

Editorial Board:
Frances Bellarsi, Université Libre de Bruxelles, Belgium
Mandy Bloomfield, Plymouth University, UK
Lily Chen, Shanghai Normal University, China
Christa Grewe-Volpp, University of Mannheim, Germany
Stephanie LeMenager, University of Oregon, USA
Timothy Morton, Rice University, USA
Pablo Mukherjee, University of Warwick, UK

Bloomsbury's *Environmental Cultures* series makes available to students and scholars at all levels the latest cutting-edge research on the diverse ways in which culture has responded to the age of environmental crisis. Publishing ambitious and innovative literary ecocriticism that crosses disciplines, national boundaries, and media, books in the series explore and test the challenges of ecocriticism to conventional forms of cultural study.

Titles available:
Bodies of Water, Astrida Neimanis
Cities and Wetlands, Rod Giblett
Civil Rights and the Environment in African-American Literature,
1895–1941, John Claborn
Climate Change Scepticism, Greg Garrard, George Handley, Axel Goodbody,
Stephanie Posthumus
Climate Crisis and the 21st-Century British Novel, Astrid Bracke
Colonialism, Culture, Whales, Graham Huggan
Ecocriticism and Italy, Serenella Iovino
Fuel, Heidi C. M. Scott

Literature as Cultural Ecology, Hubert Zapf
Nerd Ecology, Anthony Lioi
The New Nature Writing, Jos Smith
The New Poetics of Climate Change, Matthew Griffiths
This Contentious Storm, Jennifer Mae Hamilton
Climate Change Scepticism, Greg Garrard, Axel Goodbody, George
B. Handley and Stephanie Posthumus
Ecospectrality, Laura White
Teaching Environmental Writing, Isabel Galleymore
Radical Animism, Jemma Deer
Cognitive Ecopoetics, Sharon Lattig
Digital Vision and Ecological Aesthetic, Lisa FitzGerald
Environmental Cultures in Soviet East Europe, Anna Barcz
Weathering Shakespeare Evelyn O'Malley
The Living World, Samantha Walton

Forthcoming Titles:
Imagining the Plains of Latin America, Axel Pérez Trujillo Diniz
Ecocriticism and Turkey, Meliz Ergin

Ecocollapse Fiction and Cultures of Human Extinction

Sarah E. McFarland

BLOOMSBURY ACADEMIC
LONDON • NEW YORK • OXFORD • NEW DELHI • SYDNEY

BLOOMSBURY ACADEMIC
Bloomsbury Publishing Plc
50 Bedford Square, London, WC1B 3DP, UK
1385 Broadway, New York, NY 10018, USA
29 Earlsfort Terrace, Dublin 2, Ireland

BLOOMSBURY, BLOOMSBURY ACADEMIC and the Diana logo are
trademarks of Bloomsbury Publishing Plc

First published in Great Britain 2021
This paperback edition published 2022

Copyright © Sarah E. McFarland, 2021

Sarah E. McFarland has asserted her right under the Copyright, Designs
and Patents Act, 1988, to be identified as Author of this work.

For legal purposes the Acknowledgments on p. viii–x constitute an extension
of this copyright page.

Cover design: Burge Agency
Cover image: © Shutterstock

A catalogue record for this book is available from the British Library.

Library of Congress Cataloging-in-Publication Data
Names: McFarland, Sarah E., author.
Title: Ecocollapse fiction and cultures of human extinction / Sarah E. McFarland.
Description: London ; New York : Bloomsbury Academic, 2021. |
Series: Environmental cultures | Includes bibliographical references and index.
Identifiers: LCCN 2020040930 (print) | LCCN 2020040931 (ebook) |
ISBN 9781350177642 (hardback) | ISBN 9781350177659 (ebook) |
ISBN 9781350177666 (epub)
Subjects: LCSH: American fiction–21st century–History and criticism. |
Dystopias in literature. | Human ecology in literature. | Climatic changes in literature.
Classification: LCC PS374.D96 M43 2021 (print) | LCC PS374.D96 (ebook) |
DDC 813/.609372–dc23
LC record available at https://lccn.loc.gov/2020040930
LC ebook record available at https://lccn.loc.gov/2020040931

ISBN: HB: 978-1-3501-7764-2
PB: 978-1-3502-0290-0
ePDF: 978-1-3501-7765-9
eBook: 978-1-3501-7766-6

Series: Environmental Cultures

Typeset by Newgen KnowledgeWorks Pvt. Ltd., Chennai, India

To find out more about our authors and books visit www.bloomsbury.com
and sign up for our newsletters.

Contents

Acknowledgments

Many years in the making, this book slowly developed as I navigated unresolvable grief. More than a decade ago, I was appalled by scholarly condemnation of the mother's decision to die by suicide in Cormac McCarthy's *The Road* and the elevation of the father in that novel to heroic status. In response, I began writing an analysis of her death from a feminist perspective that became a project about fictional accounts of individuality within the much larger issue of mass extinction: the personal response to a global, multispecies crisis. But death by suicide as a fictional occurrence is one thing, and what was an intellectual scholarly project became blindingly, devastatingly real when my eldest child, Skye, died by suicide while at university. An unimaginable, incomprehensible loss of a vivid, beautiful existence in the world. For months I would watch the sun rise and wonder how the earth continued to turn like nothing had changed in the universe. How could so many birds help sing each morning into being with Skye no longer here? It was inconceivable to me.

This book is thus deeply informed by my own process of personal transformation within myriad grievings. I am also cognizant that there are many kinds of suffering and trauma relevant to the issues of loss amid ecocollapse. The Anthropocene and its climate effects are not distributed evenly: Nicholas Mirzoeff argues that "the Anthropocene" should rightly be called the "White Supremacy Scene," its beginning marked by massive colonial genocide. The dimensions of race, gender, class, place, dis/ability, and so many other factors mean ecocollapse affects individuals differently, in the form of sudden climate events and in the "slow violence" identified in Rob Nixon's work. Such suffering is real, personal, actual: traumas that become explicit in the fictions explored in this book. For people of privilege living in high-carbon societies, myself included, the many warnings from climate scientists should have particular resonance but so far have not resulted in a systemic paradigm shift outside of a few areas of regional progress, mostly in Europe. I kept present Zadie Smith's exhortation to "sing an elegy for the washed away! For the cycles of life, for the saltwater marshes, the houses, the humans" in her essay "Elegy for a Country's Seasons." So much is being lost. Regardless of the angle of perspective and however you look at it: we are each variously culpable and differently vulnerable, and our private worlds can collapse at any moment. Waiting for personal catastrophe or global ecocollapse to have individual effect, if it has not already, is to miss the point. Such loss is not in the future but is reality for hundreds of millions of humans and uncountable other species every day. The world has and always will be uncertain, forever. Yet while it might be full of horrors, it is also full of beauty, the lights visible in the night sky exquisite reminders of our infinitesimal circumstances. While categorizing human extinction in ecocollapse fiction, then, this book also identifies characters' various acts of personal resilience and emphatic empathy in hopes that we can face collapses of ecological and cultural certainty with courage, and together.

Early versions of some parts of this book were published elsewhere, and the author and publisher gratefully acknowledge the permission granted to reproduce the copyright material in this book. Portions of Chapter 3 previously appeared in "'Just Meat on Legs': The Last Stragglers of Climate Apocalypse" in *ISLE: Interdisciplinary Studies in Literature and Environment* 26.4 (Autumn 2019): 864–81; some passages in Chapter 2 appeared in "Animal Studies, Literary Animals, and Yann Martel's *Life of Pi*" in *The Cambridge Companion to Literature and the Environment*, edited by Louise Westling (New York: Cambridge University Press, 2014) and are reprinted with permission.

Grateful thanks to those who supported me through the joys and difficulties of writing about these complex issues and all those who pondered cannibalism, extinction, and the ends of so many worlds with me. Lively ASLE and SLSA communities provided opportunities to share my nascent work about species extinction and cannibalism with folks who have similar concerns about our planet's future and who pushed me to think more deeply about the ways that human exceptionalism works to inculcate climate change denial. I am indebted to colleagues at Northwestern State University: Jacqueline Hawkins in Watson Library's Interlibrary Loan Department facilitated my access to otherwise-unavailable materials with humor and creativity. Without her unwavering dedication to locating countless sources for me, this book could not be written. Members of the Scribblers research and writing group were enthusiastic about my passion for cannibalism and early chapter drafts: special thanks to Helaine Razovsky and Thomas Reynolds for helping me sharpen my thinking and tighten my prose. Graduate assistant Lauren Aldritch assisted with reference checks during the final stretch of manuscript production. Bloomsbury editors Ben Doyle and Lucy Brown were an absolute pleasure to work with; thanks also to the external readers for their insightful feedback and enthusiastic support. For always holding space, I am forever indebted to Jennie Joiner and Alison Langdon, who provide the most nourishing, irreverent, and gleeful friendships through years, across miles, no matter what.

To my family I owe the most heartfelt appreciation: to love is to be deeply intertwined in knotty, delightful, vulnerable ways, and my family's support marks these pages more vividly than any ink possibly could. I am immensely lucky: my parents taught me to wonder, think, and cherish, and I am grateful for all the ways their care continues to sustain me. David McFarland was unable to see this work in print, but his encouragement to not let it molder in a drawer still rings in my ears; Lois McFarland has helped guide me in more ways than she could possibly know and that I can never sufficiently articulate: thank you.

How marvelous that I get to navigate the world alongside the wise and witty Mark Melder, who buoys and anchors with his companionship, humor, and endless knowledge of the ecosystems with which we are entangled. Our son, Griffin, is profoundly inquisitive, hysterically funny, and yet somehow stoically equanimous. He radiates brilliance, and my world would never be the same without his light in it. Because words can't express my always and forever to starshine Skye and Griffin, *mo chroí*, I'll just say: this was ever for you.

1

The World Unravels

A global climate crisis is underway, and species are going extinct worldwide. The United Nations Secretary-General Antonio Guterres announced at the end of July 2019 that "This year alone, we have seen temperature records shattered from New Delhi to Anchorage, from Paris to Santiago, from Adelaide to the Arctic Circle."[1] Unpredictable shifts in formerly stable weather dynamics have touched every ecosystem, and even if we somehow managed as a species to switch to a completely zero-carbon footprint, the planet's life will still be in dire conditions for generations to come. From a wildlife standpoint, there is only grim news: the United Nations' Intergovernmental Science-Policy Platform on Biodiversity and Ecosystem Services (IPBES) Report published in May 2019 warned that one million species are at risk of extinction:

> The average abundance of native species in most major land-based habitats has fallen by at least 20%, mostly since 1900. More than 40% of amphibian species, almost 33% of reef-forming corals and more than a third of all marine mammals are threatened. The picture is less clear for insect species, but available evidence supports a tentative estimate of 10% being threatened. At least 680 vertebrate species had been driven to extinction since the 16th century and more than 9% of all domesticated breeds of mammals used for food and agriculture had become extinct by 2016, with at least 1,000 more breeds still threatened.[2]

[1] Quoted in Brady Dennis and Andrew Freedman, "Here's How the Hottest Month in Recorded History Unfolded Around the World," *The Washington Post*, August 5, 2019.
[2] "UN Report: Nature's Dangerous Decline 'Unprecedented'; Species Extinction Rates 'Accelerating,'" May 6, 2019, https://www.un.org/sustainabledevelopment/blog/2019/05/nature-decline-unprecedented-report/.

Not only are species "declining globally at rates unprecedented in human history,"[3] but we are currently undergoing what appears to be the second-fastest extinction event in the earth's history, behind only the Cretaceous–Tertiary (K–T) extinction event that famously killed off the dinosaurs (together with 75 percent of all plant and animal species) sixty-six million years ago. Yet species conservation efforts are inadequate. "It would theoretically be possible," biologists Paul Ehrlich and Anne Ehrlich argue, "to lose no more species diversity at all and yet, because of declines in population diversity, suffer such a steep decline in ecosystem services that humanity itself would go extinct."[4] Because of feedback loops in the chemistry of global warming, increasingly catastrophic floods, droughts, hurricanes, blizzards, and tornadoes will amplify climate transformations in the frightening near-future where humans and other animals face further increasing temperatures, rising waters, shifts in growing seasons, food and water shortages, disease, overcrowding, and massive loss of life. As David Wallace-Wells writes in *The Uninhabitable Earth: Life after Warming*, "We have already exited the state of environmental conditions that allowed the human animal to evolve in the first place, in an unsure and unplanned bet on just what that animal can endure. The climate system that raised us, and raised everything we now know as human culture and civilization, is now, like a parent, dead."[5] Our species may go extinct, a possibility that demands we accept and embody our worldly entanglements before individuals can begin to imagine and adapt to their potential experience of that diminishing future.

Yet climate change fiction as a genre of apocalyptic and post-apocalyptic writing has resisted facing the potentiality of human species extinction, following instead traditional generic conventions that display a predilection for happy endings by imagining primitivist communities of human survivors with the means of escaping the consequences of global climate change. In her call for "more [literary] climate change," Lucy Burnett wonders, "Is the assumption that we might somehow *solve* climate change not the apotheosis

[3] Ibid.
[4] Paul Ehrlich and Anne Ehrlich, *One with Ninevah: Politics, Consumption, and the Human Future* (Washington, DC: Island Press, 2004), 53.
[5] David Wallace-Wells, *The Uninhabitable Earth: Life after Warming* (New York: Tim Duggan Books, 2019), 18.

of the human hubris that got us into this situation in the first place?"[6] At issue, then, is how to reject the impulse of human exceptionalism that pervades Western thought and much speculative fiction by exploring those few texts that engage with the potential of human species extinction: the subject of this book. William E. Connolly describes human exceptionalism as "the idea that we are either the one species favored and nourished by a God or an unprotected species so superior to other forces and beings that we can deploy them endlessly for our purposes."[7] Human exceptionalism is imbricated within the discourse of progressivism, a symptom of how Darwin's evolutionary concept is enlisted in support of a view of progress with humans at the apex of evolutionary innovation. Evolution is, in fact, indifferent. Becoming attuned to the inseparability of human and nonhuman worlds—what Donna Haraway calls "entanglement"—thus insubstantiates the exceptionalism experienced as part of the Western human tradition. Alexis Shotwell invokes Haraway to observe that such entanglement is inescapable, "even when we cannot track or directly perceive this entanglement. It is hard for us to examine our connection with *unbearable pasts* with which we might reckon better, our implication in *impossibly complex presents* through which we might craft different modes of response, and our aspirations for *different futures* toward which we might shape different worlds-yet-to-come."[8] As Kari Weil argues, "The ethical must grow instead out of an experience of shared mortality or bodily vulnerability that is, as [Cora] Diamond writes, 'painful to think.'"[9] Because as pervasive as media-populated scientific warnings about global climate change have been for the past fifty years, those warnings have not succeeded in creating a transformational emotional force in the real world that moves people and governments to affect meaningful change, instead creating what has been called "apocalypse fatigue."[10] Zadie Smith points out that "It's hard to keep apocalypse

[6] Lucy Burnett, "What If: The Literary Case for More Climate Change," *ISLE: Interdisciplinary Studies in Literature and Environment* 26, no. 4 (Autumn 2019): 904. Emphasis in original.

[7] William E. Connolly, "Extinction Events and Entangled Humanism," in *After Extinction*, ed. Richard Grusin (Minneapolis: University of Minnesota Press, 2018), 10. Subsequent citations appear parenthetically in the text.

[8] Alexis Shotwell, *Against Purity: Living Ethically in Compromised Times* (Minneapolis: University of Minnesota Press, 2016), 8. Emphasis in original.

[9] Kari Weil, *Thinking Animals: Why Animal Studies Now?* (New York: Columbia University Press, 2012), xxii.

[10] For extended discussions of apocalypse fatigue, see Claire Gardner, "The Apocalypse Is Easy: Limitations of Our Climate Change Imaginings," *Demos*, September 13, 2015; Per Espen Stoknes, *What We Think about When We Try Not to Think about Global Warming*

consistently in mind, especially if you want to get out of bed in the morning,"[11] reminding us that the many and complex challenges of climate apocalypse make it increasingly difficult to resist a kind of purposeful obliviousness as an alternative to impotent, resigned fatalism.

Even after Darwin's evolutionary theory forced humans to accept that we are related by descent to other animals, we have maintained a polite fiction that preserves a comfortable distance, entrenching human exceptionalism within humanist philosophies and environmentalisms: humans are intelligent and extraordinary, and therefore, our species will survive the consequences of ecological exploitation, a deeply experienced anthropocentrism that is hard to counter. In Western cultures, Giorgio Agamben demonstrates, "humanity" is characterized as a dualism that discloses both what he calls "vegetative" life (that which provides biological survival) and "relational" life (that which connects with the external world). The distinction between the animal body and "the human" remains forever in flux, a "mobile border within living man [*sic*]," yet the separation between humans and all other animals is required for the definitional clarity that enables human exceptionalism: "Without this intimate caesura," Agamben writes, "the very decision of what is human and what is not would probably not be possible."[12] Global climate change and mass extinction, however, make the imbrication of the human as an animal abundantly clear. Definitional dualisms become irrelevant; humans are nonetheless animals, as embroiled in climate change as any other creature. Thus far, though, human exceptionalism triumphs in discourses about global climate change. Madeleine Fagan argues in "Who's Afraid of the Ecological Apocalypse?" that "the apocalyptic framing of climate change is at least in some instances expressly intended to galvanise action on ecological matters" but, as she goes on to prove, has been successful instead at reproducing non-relational subjects "because the range of possible answers to [questions about the world and the

---

(Vermont: Chelsea Green Publishing, 2015); and Ted Nordhaus and Michael Shellenberger, "Apocalypse Fatigue: Losing the Public on Climate Change," *Yale Environment 360*, November 16, 2009. In *Being Ecological* (Cambridge, MA: MIT Press, 2018), Timothy Morton justifiably calls the "information dump" that even I could not resist at the beginning of this chapter part of what makes "being ecological" so complicated.

[11]   From Zadie Smith, "Elegy for a Country's Seasons," *New York Review of Books* 61, no. 6 (April 3, 2014): 6.

[12]   Giorgio Agamben, *The Open: Man and Animal*, trans. Kevin Attell (Stanford: Stanford University Press, 2004), 15.

place of the human within it] is already mapped out; 'we' are either individuals distinct from nature and from future generations or part of a universal whole undifferentiated across time and space."[13] Climate change marks "a finite space in which 'we' are now all joined in a tragedy of the commons," as Claire Colebrook demonstrates, although Dipesh Chakrabarty rightly interrogates the notion of a human "species" given that the causes and consequences of climate change are unequally distributed. Furthermore, he writes, "We humans never experience ourselves as a species. We can only intellectually comprehend or infer the existence of the human species but never experience it as such. . . . One never experiences being a concept."[14] Uncovering the operations of economic power and the globalization of capitalism that are at the root of carbon-fueled climate change, he proposes a new universalism[15] because, as Ursula K. Heise explains, "climate change threatens *all* modes of humans' inhabitation of the planet . . . and thereby highlights boundary conditions of humans' collective existence that are unrelated."[16] Following these scholars and in pursuit of an argument that breaks down human exceptionalism, my use of "we" throughout is done with explicit acknowledgment of the knot of ethical dilemmas around who and what is included and excluded in various "we" formulations and the conflicting precarities, vulnerabilities, and diverse human and nonhuman populations of the world. I reference the human species in its entirety while recognizing that there exists considerable diversity within such a unifying pronoun. But in what other way can we imagine our species' extinction if not as individual members of that cohort of animals? As Heise explains, "The notion of the Anthropocene brings with it the idea that the human species is a collective with geological force, a natural condition for the rest of life on the planet."[17] In *Exposed: Environmental Politics and Pleasures in Posthuman*

---

[13] Madeleine Fagan, "Who's Afraid of the Ecological Apocalypse? Climate Change and the Production of the Ethical Subject," *The British Journal of Politics and International Relations* 19, no. 2 (2017): 229, 237. Subsequent citations appear parenthetically in the text.

[14] Dipesh Chakrabarty, "The Climate of History: Four Theses," *Critical Inquiry* 35, no. 2 (Winter 2009): 220.

[15] Nicholas Mirzoeff valuably problematizes this "new universal history" in "It's Not the Anthropocene, It's the White Supremacy Scene; or, The Geological Color Line," in *After Extinction*, ed. Richard Grusin (Minneapolis: University of Minnesota Press, 2018), 123–49.

[16] Ursula K. Heise, *Imagining Extinction: The Cultural Meanings of Endangered Species* (Chicago, IL: University of Chicago Press, 2016), 221. Emphasis in original. For a comprehensive analysis of Chakrabarty's "new universalism" and the scholarly debate that took place prior to her book's publication in 2016, see Heise, *Imagining Extinction*, 220–6.

[17] Heise, *Imagining Extinction*, 221.

Times, Stacy Alaimo illustrates trans-corporeal intermeshings to show that "Thinking the human as a species does not preclude analysis and critique of economic systems, environmental devastation and social injustice."[18]

Accordingly, authors continue to imagine climate-changed futures and conjure realistic characters who struggle to adapt and construct lives and deaths worth living and dying. Nonfiction books have become increasingly urgent about global environmental devastation: Naomi Klein warns of climate barbarism in *On Fire* (2019), Robert Bringhurst and Jan Zwicky recommend moral virtues in *Learning to Die: Wisdom in the Age of Climate Crisis* (2018), Anna Lowenhaupt Tsing suggests accepting precarity in *The Mushroom at the End of the World* (2015), Roy Scranton portends the extinction of civilization in *Learning to Die in the Anthropocene* (2015), Craig Childs offers a field guide to the *Apocalyptic Planet* (2013), Julian Cribb cautions of *The Coming Famine* (2010), Orrin Pilkey and Rob Young warn of *The Rising Sea* (2009), Peter Ward alerts us to *The Flooded Earth* (2010), Alan Weisman imagines *The World Without Us* (2007),[19] and so on. Likewise, fictional narratives about global ecological disasters have been the topic of science fiction since before the Cold War fears of nuclear apocalypse, were reimagined in the 1960s with the publication of Rachel Carson's *Silent Spring*, and have continued to be a popular genre since then in print and on film. They fascinate us because end-of-the-world accounts can "provide both the voyeuristic satisfaction of terrible violence and the Robinson Crusoe excitement of starting over again," as Claire P. Curtis puts it.[20] In science fiction especially, Lisa Garforth argues, the post-catastrophe scenario "has often been used to explore the possibility of non-repressive, communitarian societies emerging from the ruins of advanced modernity, wherein a simpler and richer good life thrives away from the shadow of technology, the city, and global industrial capitalism."[21] Slavoj Žižek reveals that such utopian projects do not eliminate evil, however: they

[18] Stacy Alaimo, *Exposed: Environmental Politics and Pleasures in Posthuman Times* (Minneapolis: University of Minnesota Press, 2016), 155. For her critique of what she calls Chakrabarty's retreat from bodily materiality, see *Exposed*, 148–56.

[19] For a detailed interrogation of environmental nonfiction narratives that vanish the human species, see Greg Garrard, "Worlds without Us: Some Types of Disanthropy," *SubStance* 41 (2012): 40–60.

[20] Claire P. Curtis, *Postapocalyptic Fiction and the Social Contract: "We'll Not Go Home Again"* (Lanham, MD: Lexington Books, 2010), 6.

[21] Lisa Garforth, "Green Utopias: Beyond Apocalypse, Progress, and Pastoral," *Utopian Studies* 16, no. 3 (2005): 399.

convert it into some "mythic threat" against which the community establishes itself.[22] By being both "human-caused" and "natural," climate change permits a literary opportunity to manifest the kind of catastrophic imagery that utilizes tropes from both the horrors of human-made Frankenstein myths (like nuclear destruction) and those myths of crisis with cosmic or natural origins (asteroids, volcanoes, and the like) made compelling in these generic conventions, tracing, to use Andrew Tate's description, "the contradictory desires for self-destruction and survival that haunt human beings."[23] Climate change "has now eclipsed nuclear terror as the prime mover of the apocalyptic and dystopian imagination," Rowland Hughes and Pat Wheeler observe.[24] But what happens when there is no chance for redemption, when the means necessary for species survival are no longer available?

This book examines what happens when there is no happy ending—when the means to survive as a fully fleshed human being no longer exist—through the practice of accounting for the intra-actions between co-constitutive creatures (human and nonhuman) in ways that eschew human exceptionalism. My argument is that twenty-first-century realistic fiction incorporating the effects of ecocollapse results in a much more radically multiplicitious and diverse view of what it means to be "human" in a climate-changed world only when there is no redemptive ending. Following Margaret Atwood's description from *In Other Worlds*, I examine literature in which "things that really could happen but just hadn't completely happened"[25] are realistically speculated. I use the term "ecocollapse" rather than "climate fiction" because climate fiction is defined so as to emphasize the explicit engagement with anthropogenic climate change *regardless of other genre elements*. Gregers Anderson defines "cli-fi" as "fictions that explicitly use humanity's emissions of greenhouse gasses as some kind of driver in their world-making."[26] Antonia Mehnert defines it as those "works that explicitly engage with anthropogenic

22 Slavoj Žižek, *The Plague of Fantasies* (London: Verso, 1997), 32.
23 Andrew Tate, *Apocalyptic Fiction* (London: Bloomsbury Academic, 2017), 22. Subsequent citations appear parenthetically in the text.
24 Rowland Hughes and Pat Wheeler, "Eco-dystopias: Nature and the Dystopian Imagination," *Critical Survey* 25, no. 2 (2013): 1.
25 Margaret Atwood, *In Other Worlds: SF and the Human Imagination* (London: Doubleday, 2011), 6.
26 Gregers Anderson, "Cli-Fi and the Uncanny," *ISLE: Interdisciplinary Studies in Literature and Environment* 23, no. 4 (Autumn 2016): 856.

climate change [wherein] meteorological phenomena do not just provide the backdrop setting against which the story unfolds; climate change significantly alters and is a prevalent issue for characters, plot, and setting."[27] Although many of the works explored in these pages are "consciously and explicitly engaged with anthropogenic climate change," to use Matthew Schneider-Mayerson's description of climate fiction,[28] I here prioritize realism, diminished ecosystems, and hopeless endings. Accordingly, I am labeling "realistic ecocollapse fiction" that which engages with vastly diminished ecosystems, regardless of their cause, to account for manifestations of what Timothy Clark describes as "hairline cracks in the familiar life-worlds, at the local and personal scale of each individual life,"[29] as those cracks deepen in futuristic accounts and result in human extinction rather than community renewal.

The novels I analyze are twenty-first-century speculations of human extinction that are "realistic," then, in the sense that they imagine a future world without interventions of as-yet uninvented technology, interplanetary travel, alien invasion, or other science fiction elements that leave hope for rescue or long-term survival. They build ecocollapsed earth worlds that are scientifically probable in the Anthropocene. Thus this book documents what Richard Kerridge has argued "we are collectively evading" in our resistance to "explor[ing] the emotional complexity of our responses to the threat" of extinction as an end point.[30] Amitav Ghosh asks in *The Great Derangement: Climate Fiction and the Unthinkable*, "What is it about climate change that the mention of it should lead to banishment from the preserves of serious fiction? And what does this tell us about culture writ large and its patterns of evasion?"[31] He argues that climate change's absence is reflective of an unwillingness to confront the Anthropocene because of its scale,

---

[27] Antonia Mehnert, *Climate Change Fictions: Representations of Global Warming in American Literature* (Switzerland: Palgrave Macmillan, 2016), 38.

[28] Matthew Schneider-Mayerson, "Climate Change Fiction," in *American Literature in Transition, 2000–2010*, ed. Rachel Greenwald Smith (Cambridge, MA: Cambridge University Press, 2017), 312.

[29] Timothy Clark, *Ecocriticism on the Edge: The Anthropocene as a Threshold Concept* (London: Bloomsbury Academic, 2015), 9. Subsequent citations appear parenthetically in the text.

[30] Richard Kerridge, "The Single Source," *Ecozon@* 1, no. 1 (2010): 159. doi: 10.37536/ECOZONA.2010.1.1.334.

[31] Amitav Ghosh, *The Great Derangement: Climate Change and the Unthinkable* (Chicago, IL: University of Chicago Press, 2017), 11.

pervasiveness, and dreadful implications.[32] By uncovering examples of human extinction, then, I show how some authors resist denial, although their works are chosen not only because they are literary creations of human extinction—which is remarkable in itself—but because they illustrate the ethical stakes and imbrication of what Haraway calls "naturecultures" as coevolutionary. With its close examination of realistic ecocollapse fictions that reveal an end to the human subject, this book documents a different analytic than that of other climate change explorations like E. Ann Kaplan's *Climate Trauma* (2016), which illustrates what she calls "pretraumatic stress disorder" in films; Antonia Mehnert's *Climate Change Fictions* (2016), which attends to various political, economic, social, and cultural processes of anthropogenic climate change in science fiction and thrillers and explicitly focuses on novels that promote hope; Adam Trexler's *Anthropocene Fictions* (2015), which inventories a wide range of science fiction texts; Kate Rigby's *Dancing with Disaster* (2015), which theorizes the material-discursive practices of historical eco-catastrophic events; and Andrew Tate's *Apocalyptic Fiction* (2017), which explores various kinds of human self-destruction and survival across a number of genres. My analysis resonates with Pramod K. Nayar's concept of ecoprecarity in *Ecoprecarity: Vulnerable Lives in Literature and Culture* (2019), which glosses specific types of ecological vulnerability in science fiction and film; he argues that "ecological disaster and eco-apocalypse along with different states of ecoprecarity are central to contemporary 'environmentality,'" following Lawrence Buell.[33] However, Nayar's work interrogates numerous science fiction, fantasy, and other dystopian novels and films to illustrate the condition itself: to identify its common features. He applies Judith Butler's notion of precarious lives while purposefully disregarding whether that precariousness is "threatening or as potential for new beginnings."[34] In contrast, I am interested in what happens if humanity's existential crisis comes to its logical conclusion, and thus I provide a deep analysis of the few realistic ecocollapse fictions that do not ratify generic conventions of

---

[32] It is important to note that Ghosh narrowly defines the archetypal novels of his study so as to exclude futuristic, science fiction, fantasy, magical realism, and other genres that do not address the Anthropocene "actually happening on earth, at this time" (27) in *The Great Derangement*.

[33] Pramod K. Nayar, *Ecoprecarity: Vulnerable Lives in Literature and Culture* (New York: Routledge, 2019), 7.

[34] Ibid., 11.

species survival: the hopeless endings are the point. I argue that forecasting human extinction necessitates coming to terms with the complex mapping of ecosystems, global warming, and human and nonhuman cultures to exert pressure on human exceptionalism's contradictions, exclusions, repressions, and marginalizations to welcome what emerges through the incoherences in exceptionalist thinking. Climate scientists' dire warnings that the world we take for granted is undergoing dramatic and potentially devastating changes have largely been resisted, but perhaps, now that those changes are on display globally and in every newspaper, we can turn to literature to see some ways authors have realistically speculated human extinction in ecocollapsed worlds. What can the humanities teach us about our species' co-emergence with the Anthropocene? What might it be like to go extinct?

Ecocollapse Fiction

Several features distinguish apocalyptic and post-apocalyptic fictions from the larger genre of science fiction, although there is some fluidity between the two: those categorized as "apocalypse" emphasize the destruction of the world and not the aftermath, whereas those categorized as "post-apocalypse" feature the aftermath and starting over instead of focusing on the source of whatever crisis brought down civilization. Robert MacFarlane observes that "It is the central paradox of catastrophe fiction that to destroy the world you must first summon it into being,"[35] writing a world in which the catastrophe is instigated by either human hubris or natural causes. Traditionally in post-apocalyptic fiction, the main character is a man who somehow survives the catastrophic event and becomes the heroic leader of a group of "good" survivors. While satisfying their basic needs for food, shelter, and other logistical requirements for bodily survival, the group encounters "bad" others and eventually must respond with violence to outside threats to their newly formed community. As Eugene Thacker puts it, "In spite of the disaster, the human emerges even

---

[35] Robert MacFarlane, Introduction to *The Crystal World*, by J. G. Ballard (New York: Picador, 2018), xii.

stronger than it was before, with survival becoming a form of heroism."[36] The respectable group's final success illustrates the rise of civilization and humanity from the ashes of destruction and leaves readers with both an instructional message of warning and a sense of hope. Although writing specifically about films, Susan Sontag explains the lure of apocalyptic and post-apocalyptic themes in "The Imagination of Disaster," arguing that "alongside the hopeful fantasy of moral simplification and international unity embodied in the science fiction films lurk the deepest anxieties about contemporary existence" and "the condition of the individual psyche."[37] These subjects reflect the modern, global anxieties of the twentieth and twenty-first centuries: as Tate illustrates, "The apocalyptic tradition is sometimes highly misanthropic; the earth, it suggests, would be in better condition if *Homo sapiens* were no longer around" (132). Nonetheless, these narratives inevitably result in a positive outcome.

Stephen King's commercially popular, mainstream novel *The Stand* (also adapted into a television miniseries) is a familiar case in point in which all the traditional features of the genre play a role, including the possibility of a happy ending. The catastrophe is twofold: the first is the human-made biological weapon with a 99 percent mortality rate devised by the US military and accidentally unleashed when the fail-safes fail; the second is the final spiritual and physical battle between good and evil. Although there are several major characters, the main character is a righteous man named Stuart who leads a misfit band against the evil Randall Flagg, as representative of Mother Abagail and all that is virtuous in the world against all that is malevolent. As is true in most works of the genre, good and evil are explicitly represented: Stuart means "house guardian," Abagail "God's joy," and Randall "wolf." While the newly formed community of the Free Zone settles in Boulder, Colorado, a "rock" where the ethical survivors can take a stand in opposition to evil, Randall's community settles in Las Vegas, Nevada, otherwise known as "Sin City." Mother Abagail tells Stuart and his three companions that "God didn't bring you folks together to make a committee or a community. He brought you here only to send you further, on a quest. He means for you to try and destroy

[36] Eugene Thacker, "Notes on Extinction and Existence," *Configurations* 20, nos. 1–2 (Winter–Spring 2012): 139–40.
[37] Susan Sontag, "The Imagination of Disaster," in *Against Interpretation and Other Essays* (New York: Dell, 1979), 220.

this Dark Prince,"[38] so they travel to Las Vegas to do battle with Flagg and his followers for the symbolic salvation of surviving humankind. Evil, in the form of Flagg, is an independent entity that takes advantage of human mistakes and unfortunate situations to foster more malicious behavior. The final conflict is a collision of hate and love, destruction and creation, murderousness and compassion, selfishness and generosity, and it takes the literal Hand of God to be resolved. In fact, as clever, complex, and richly told as most of *The Stand* is, the conflict's ending is not very satisfying. King employs what feels like a cheat: a hand-shaped light in the sky reaches down to earth and detonates a nuclear warhead, destroying Las Vegas after Flagg escapes. There is no battle. The three "good" men who arrive in Las Vegas turn themselves over to Flagg's men, are imprisoned and one is killed, and then the remaining two are put in cages to be torn apart in front of the entire "evil" community as a bonding ritual that further instills their obedience to Flagg. Although the four white knights walking to do battle with the Dark Man make a compelling story, the ending fizzles out when those knights use no strategy, employ no scheme, order no attack: they are simply sent to be a blood sacrifice, and they passively accept their role. The novel concludes with a birth in one society and the rebirth of Flagg in another because the world "always, at the end, came round to the same place again" (1439), although this ending was added to the 1990 extended version and was not included in the original, which had a happier tone. In both editions, however, we see the recreation of society and the explicit moral simplicity described by Sontag as standards of the genre.

Most fiction that situates itself in a climate-changed future also leans on the promise of species survival and social rebirth, typically signified by pregnancy or children. Trexler's *Anthropocene Fiction* documents hundreds of such examples within his larger examination of science fiction, fantasy, and other genres of post-apocalyptic climate fiction speculation. One example he does not survey that fits my definition of realistic climate change fiction for lacking science fiction elements is Clara Hume's *Back to the Garden* (2013), in which a small group of people survive warmer temperatures, disease, polluted water sources, and crushed public services on a mountain in Idaho, having

---

[38] Stephen King, *The Stand: Complete and Uncut Edition* (1990; repr., New York: Anchor Books, 2011), 1142. Subsequent citations appear parenthetically in the text.

reverted to a primitive lifestyle whereby they hunt with bows and arrows and even weave their own cloth. Their small community is contrasted with lawless thugs but grows as they add nonthreatening strangers to their group. The novel fulfills characteristics of the genre described by Tate of twenty-first-century apocalyptic fiction set after the collapse of society wherein "the ruined worlds they evoke are . . . frequently a product of our current propensities and trajectories: the legacy of the early twenty-first century to these near-future eras is often environmental degradation, consumer greed, the loss of human rights and the exploitation of future generations who will pay a high price for current folly or cruelty" (132). As is pervasive in such literature, however, that "high price" is mediated in *Back to the Garden*: hope for a sustained human future comes in the promise of one woman's pregnancy and the potential renewal of "civilization" epitomized by human reproduction within the community of "good" survivors. Nicole Seymour, applying Lee Edelman's critique of "reproductive futurism" directly to environmentalist rhetoric, writes of the "many environmental campaigns that use the image of the child" that their "sentimentalized rhetoric . . . suggests that concern for the future qua the planet can only emerge, or emerges most effectively, from white, heterosexual, familial reproductivity."[39] Furthermore, pregnancy is a convenient signifier in human exceptionalist discourse, representative of a potential future and successful survival of the species. That so many otherwise dystopian post-apocalyptic fictions end with pregnancy or birth allows readers the emotional security of posterity itself.

Most instances of the climate fiction artistic form, then, offer a future to their characters that is worthy of the thing experienced as a fully fledged and recognizable "life"—a continuity of relationships between human subjects, "overdetermined, an extension of us" in the words of Madeleine Fagan (236). They model a type of "nature nostalgia"[40] whereby the human species gets an opportunity to begin again. However, very few examples of realistic ecocollapse fiction demonstrate the opposite: the specter of climate change and

[39] Nicole Seymour, *Strange Natures: Futurity, Empathy, and the Queer Ecological Imagination* (Chicago: University of Illinois Press, 2013), 7.
[40] This is Catriona Mortimer-Sandilands's term; see her "Melancholy Natures, Queer Ecologies," in *Queer Ecologies: Sex, Nature, Politics, Desire*, ed. Mortimer-Sandilands and Bruce Erickson (Bloomington: Indiana University Press, 2010), 331–58.

the concomitant ecological collapse profoundly threaten the sovereignty of the human subject, so the post-apocalyptic scenario is one of human extinction, not a rebirth of society. The chapters that follow trace the confrontation of extinction amid ecological devastation in these realistic speculative fictions, interrogating the effects of changing environments to uncover how this category of literature imagines our collective species' final end, responding to Clark's demand that ecocritics "engage more directly with delusions of self-importance" (198). Several patterns become apparent: ecocollapse can be the central cause of depopulation, resulting in food shortages, water issues, and a slow and painful extinction wrought with fears about cannibalism and violence; or climate change can be a secondary factor after disease, often brought about by warming environments, first depopulates the world, leaving survivors similarly facing resource depletion, cannibalism, and species extinction. Regardless, denatured ecosystems traumatize characters by severing them from important connections to their ethical frameworks in ways that further decenter human exceptionalism. The murder, death, or absence of human infants in these novels, as I uncover in the chapters that follow, transforms from emotive tragedy or parental failure into ecological awareness: these worlds cannot sustain the human futures symbolized by new births. Finally, my "last witness" contention enriches existing analyses of these complex issues by foregrounding human extinction.

Cannibalism

The specter of cannibalism runs through these texts and is crucial to boundary-making and -breaking practices in ecocollapsed futures, where chaos and food scarcity turn any available flesh to food and redefine traditional ideas about us/them tribalisms. Sebastian Junger even defines one's "tribe" as "the people you feel compelled to share the last of your food with,"[41] foregrounding the necessity of material sustenance and the enmeshed issues raised by cannibalism as a practice. From ancient Greek myths to twenty-first-century

---

[41]   Sebastian Junger, *Tribe: On Homecoming and Belonging* (New York: Twelve Hachette Books, 2016), xvii.

post-apocalyptic novels, cannibalism proliferates, forcing the reconsideration of dichotomous thinking about "self" and "other," a civilized "us" and a savage "them" and the elision of that difference. As Maggie Kilgour argues in *From Communion to Cannibalism*, "Incorporation—the most basic example of which is eating—depends upon and enforces an absolute division between inside and outside; but in the act itself that opposition disappears, dissolving the structure it appears to produce."[42] What, then, when the food being eaten is human flesh? Montaigne famously observed that "Everyone calls barbarism that which is not his own usage."[43] Cannibalism was once thought to be a nearly universal human taboo, and yet anthropophagy has been a fact of our *Homo* species history: a convincing amount of evidence examined by various genetic scientists, archeologists, paleoanthropologists, and other researchers indicates that cannibalism was widespread among prehistoric humans. The oldest evidence of cannibalism comes from a French cave called Moula-Guercy, where 100,000-year-old skeletal remains indicate that human ancestors defleshed the bones and extracted brains and marrow from members of their own species.[44] Some 50,000 years later, Neanderthals were cannibalizing each other, as evidenced by the findings in a cave at El Sidron, Spain.[45] Modern humans carry genes that protect against diseases contracted by eating contaminated brain tissue that, according to researchers, are genetic links to cannibalism and add more depth to the already wide body of evidence for prehistoric human cannibalism.[46] But humans did not stop in prehistory. As Bill Schutt demonstrates in *Cannibalism: A Perfectly Natural History* (2017), it is an almost ordinary occurrence; similarly, Richard Sugg reveals that even the stuffy Victorians ate human body parts as medical curatives in his *Mummies, Cannibals and Vampires: The History of Corpse Medicine from the Renaissance to the Victorians* (2016). Add ritualized cannibalism in

---

[42] Maggie Kilgour, *From Communion to Cannibalism: An Anatomy of Metaphors of Incorporation* (Princeton, NJ: Princeton University Press, 1990), 4.

[43] Michel de Montaigne, "Of Cannibals," in *The Essays of Michel de Montaigne*, vol. 1, trans. Jacob Zeitlin (New York: Knopf, 1934), 181.

[44] Alban DeFleur, et al., "Neanderthal Cannibalism at Moula-Guercy, Ardeche, France," *Science* 286, no. 5437 (October 1, 1999): 128–31.

[45] Carl Zimmer, "Bones Give Peek into the Lives of Neanderthals," *The New York Times*, December 20, 2010.

[46] Simon Mead, et al., "Balancing Selection at the Prion Protein Gene Consistent with Prehistoric Kurulike Epidemics," *Science* 300, no. 5619 (April 25, 2003): 640–3.

Mesoamerica, funerary cannibalism in China, sacrificial cannibalism in Brazil, pathological cannibalism in the United States, and starvation cannibalism the world over, and we must agree with Christy G. Turner and Jacqueline A. Turner's claim that "cannibalism has occurred everywhere at one time or another"[47] prompted by various cultural, behavioral, or environmental factors.

Cannibalism is a provocative, more-than-material iteration of tribal affiliations that marks a gap between figurative and literal beingness and various groupings of distinction. Formally, anthropophagy can be categorized in several ways that are useful for considering how characters in the fictions interrogated here attempt to reify human exceptionalism and the inside/outside aspects of cannibalism. Endocannibalism, the eating of family or group members, cannot exist except in extreme situations because it would destroy the population (a group cannot survive if it eats itself to do so), but reports and claims of endocannibalism have been made throughout the ancient and modern world: as an institutionalized way to show respect for the dead, to obtain power from a sacrificial victim, and of course as associated with psychopathology (the award-winning television show *Hannibal* is a visually beautiful and ethically problematizing example of such). As Peggy Reeves Sanday argues in *Divine Hunger: Cannibalism as a Cultural System*, in endocannibalism, "human flesh is a physical channel for communicating social value and procreative fertility from one generation to the next among a group of humans tied to one another by virtue of sharing certain substances with common ancestors. Endocannibalism recycles and regenerates social forces that are believed to be physically constituted in bodily substances or bones at the same time that it binds the living to the dead in perpetuity."[48] Exocannibalism is a more frequent occurrence, perhaps: the eating of enemies or outsiders, those who are "other," does not reduce one's own population and thus becomes a protein or social benefit by enforcing group insider/outsider status. Japanese troops, for example, practiced cannibalism on enemy soldiers during the Second World War, sometimes cutting flesh "from living captives" despite no shortage of food, expressly to "consolidate the group

---

[47] Christy G. Turner II and Jacqueline A. Turner, *Man Corn: Cannibalism and Violence in the Prehistoric American Southwest* (Salt Lake City: University of Utah Press, 1999), 1.

[48] Peggy Reeves Sanday, *Divine Hunger: Cannibalism as a Cultural System* (Cambridge, MA: Cambridge University Press, 1986), 7.

feeling of the troops," according to Toshiyuki Tanaka.[49] Interestingly, the tribal constructions that demarcate exocannibalism are flexible and even complicate species boundaries: Australian Aborigines and Kung Bushmen (among others) "make a distinction between food dogs and non-food dogs . . . by conferring names on the latter. Once it has a name, it is no longer potential food,"[50] thus accentuating the counter-dehumanization of cannibalized humans. Within these two overarching classifications exists survival cannibalism, the emergency consumption of human flesh during wartime, famine, drought, or other food shortages to survive. While survival cannibalism is often defensible given what is otherwise certain starvation, it also comes with high social and psychological (and sometimes legal) consequences for the survivors.[51] As Jane Elliott writes, "To have to decide between cannibalism and death is appalling, but it is not a decision one can imagine facing with indifference. The extreme options and intense interest in life that characterize survival stories gesture toward one of the cruelest aspects of suffering agency—the fact that the worse the choices on offer are, the more interested in the decision the subject will tend to be."[52] None of the decisions are easy ones. In the film *Snowpiercer*, Curtis says, "No food, no water. After a month, we ate the weak. You know what I hate about myself? I know what people taste like. I know that babies taste best."[53] His self-hatred is greatest not simply because after a month without food he resorted to cannibalism, but also because he knows "that babies taste best."

By making invisible the animal bodies transformed into food, many people already disguise the violence inherent to more traditional meat eating, a system first described by Carol Adams in *The Sexual Politics of Meat* (1996). The process of dismembering and renaming animals into edible body parts makes their subjectivity and individuality an "absent referent" through which "Western culture constantly renders the material

[49] Terry McCarthy, "Japanese Troops 'Ate Flesh of Enemies and Civilians,'" *The Independent*, August 12, 1992. See also Geoff Spencer, "Japan Hears of World War II Cannibalism a Half-century Later," *The Associated Press*, August 12, 1992.
[50] Richard C. Francis, *Domesticated: Evolution in a Man-Made World* (New York: Norton, 2015), 30–1.
[51] See, for instance, Piers Paul Read's *Alive: The Story of the Andes Survivors* about the famous plane crash in 1972; survivors resorted to cannibalism and faced intense public backlash when they were finally rescued after ten weeks trapped on a mountain.
[52] Jane Elliott, "Suffering Agency: Imagining Neoliberal Personhood in North America and Britain," *Social Text* (115) 31, no. 2 (Summer 2013): 92.
[53] *Snowpiercer* (2013), [Film] Dir. Bong Joon-ho, South Korea: Moho Film.

reality of violence into controlled and controllable metaphors."[54] The death of another being is invisible on carnivorous plates through the steps of objectification, fragmentation, and consumption that turns, for example, cattle into meatloaf: "The literal process of violently transforming living animals to dead consumable ones is emblematic of the conceptual process by which the referent point of meat eating is changed," Adams argues.[55] Simply put, *objectification* is the act of treating another being as an object or thing, as not being worthy except as a means to an end, as not having control of one's own life, as not being an actor in the world, as not recognized as being a unique individual, or as not having opinions that matter. *Fragmentation* in Marx's theory of alienation is the "splintering of human nature into a number of misbegotten parts," which Sandra Lee Bartky extends to being closely identified with the body rather than the mind or personality, a person thus becoming an "object" fractured into various body parts separated from mind and personality, reduced to external appearance.[56] And finally in this process is *consumption*, whereby an objectified being's fragmented social or physical identity becomes consumed and assimilated as a product of separable parts. We most often see consumption in advertising or pornography or the treatment of sexual partners as conquests, but Adams connects the dehumanization of women to the objectification, fragmentation, and consumption of nonhuman animals.

Consequently, humans objectify, fragment, and consume other animals and objectify, fragment, and dehumanize each other, and I want to entangle all these ideas here, crossing the species boundary to explore what it means to eat the flesh of another human. Carnivory is marked by a rigid ideological commitment to the division between humans and other animals: a categorical cut. Cannibalism erases difference by collapsing species boundaries. It breaks down the exceptionalist construction of humans as superior to all other "consumable" animals, proving that all flesh is flesh, and human meat is animal meat and tastes recognizably as such, too. According to William Seabrook,

---

[54] Carol Adams, *The Sexual Politics of Meat: A Feminist-Vegetarian Critical Theory* (New York: Continuum, 1996), 43.
[55] Ibid., 47.
[56] Sandra Lee Bartky, *Femininity and Domination: Studies in the Phenomenology of Oppression* (New York: Routledge, 1990), 31.

human flesh tastes most like veal (the undeveloped muscle of young calves). He says,

> It was mild, good meat with no other sharply defined or highly characteristic taste such as, for instance, goat, high game, and pork have. . . . The roast, from which I cut and ate a central slice, was tender, and in color, texture, smell as well as taste, strengthened my certainty that of all the meats we habitually know, veal is the one meat to which this meat is accurately comparable.[57]

The revulsion experienced while reading that a human rump tastes like baby cow flesh is part of how cannibalism, as a concept, functions to mark the eater as inhumane and the eaten as an object without human status (it is a "roast," not a person's buttock). Cannibalized flesh reveals the abject in the way we revolt violently against aspects of our being that are deemed unacceptable, denying them or projecting them onto others, even while cannibalism and carnivory exist along a blurry continuum of the absent referent in a way that transforms ethical positioning in relation to food sources as explicitly non-innocent, explicitly a relation of another's suffering, and renders any concomitant ethical categories obsolete and irrelevant. Cannibals must objectify, fragment, and consume within their own species, creating a recursive cycle that sets up absolute oppositions only to show that they are the same, that there are no differences after all. Cannibalism thus fundamentally threatens the integrity of the human self.

I argue in the chapters that follow that acts of cannibalism in the ecocollapse fictions explored here disintegrate notions of absolute difference and articulate multiple fears of anthropophagy: the fear of being cannibalized and the fear of becoming cannibal, the fear of becoming human meat and the fear of eating it. Yet cannibalism queers even these concepts of duality and replaces them with simultaneity. What follows is thus not a superficial analysis of the ways in which cannibalism appears but focuses on how the human/cannibal exists in oscillation as a confrontation with the stark inarticulable materiality of all life. In eating, as Haraway explains,

> We are most inside the differential relationalities that make us who and what we are and that materialize what we must do if response and regard are to

---

[57] William Bueller Seabrook, *Jungle Ways* (London: George G. Harrap, 1931), 172.

have any meaning . . . There is no way to eat and not kill, no way to eat and not become with other mortal beings to whom we are accountable, no way to pretend innocence and transcendence or a final peace.[58]

Rather than fallacious thinking of me/meat in oppositional terms, then, I present an explicit, unsentimental exploration of eating and extinction as representative of the problem of our status as human beings who become hungry: the specter of our common animality, which entangles humans with the rest of the world and reveals that supposedly "ethical" cultural and social structures have false durability. By preparing and eating the human body as though it is animal, the eater risks being marked inhumane by simultaneously denying the flesh its humanity. However, one cannot be a cannibal without also being human, and meat cannot be anything but human flesh to mark the consumer of it "cannibalistic." Paradoxically, then, cannibalism functions to place the cannibal both inside and outside the borders of civilization and civility, collapsing the self/other divide only to reaffirm it and only to collapse it again, entwining across any remaining category boundaries that otherwise enact human exceptionalism at points of privation and extinction.

Anxieties about cannibalistic behaviors in vastly diminished ecosystems thus figure self-identity as radically malleable, as I unpack in the following chapters. In Cormac McCarthy's *The Road* (2006), for example, the father and son repeatedly insist that they will remain "the good guys," those who do not eat other people. The otherness of the cannibals and their food is absolute for the father but ruptures in his actual experiences, as I develop in Chapter 3. Some marauders' cannibalism further amplifies fear in a recursive cycle of violence and power: the consumption of human meat terrifies and controls those who witness or fear it while providing the cannibals with protein for their continued survival and physical strength. Anthropophagy in *The Road* provides some cannibals with social and physical control of others, access to women, and access to food: standard images of savagery. Importantly, though, cannibals also demonstrate music, art, and community, and thus those groups reveal a decisive *cultural* adaptation within the barren ecosystem that is worth

---

[58] Donna Haraway, *When Species Meet* (Minneapolis: University of Minnesota Press, 2008), 295. Haraway is absolutely not advocating for cannibalism, on the off chance that is not clear. She continues: "Because eating and killing cannot be hygienically separated does *not* mean that just any way of eating and killing is fine," and she advocates for thoughtful practices of responsibility.

exploring, following Robert Redfield's point that "the rightness of what is done by other people follows from *their* view of things, not ours" in his discussions of cultural relativism.[59] In "Diary of an Interesting Year" by Helen Simpson (2012), the possibility that M might eat the unnamed narrator after using her body in so many other ways marks him as absolute other as well, in ways that careful analysis of the story problematizes. The connection between rape and other violence is not lost on the protagonist, even as readers recognize that definitive characterizations about materiality and savagery collapse in the text.

Cannibalism itself becomes indeterminate in Yann Martel's 2001 novel *Life of Pi*, where the complexity of narratives and the ultimate question of the story's stability refuses human exceptionalism and interweaves agencies of becoming in and with shared space, as I develop in Chapter 2. *Life of Pi*'s heterogeneous defiance of genre boundaries and experimentation with "truth" destabilizes lifeboat narrative conventions and creates spaces for reconsidering identity in ecocollapsed futures. I also examine novels within which characters try to counter the self-preservation instinct, those that explore what it means to be human not biologically but psychologically and spiritually, where culture in the form of art is not correlated with cannibalistic barbarity like it is in *The Road*; these characters attempt to reject dehumanizing behaviors even when the consequences might be individual death, although I problematize their concepts of ethics and humanity. When there is nothing more precious than self-preservation, how can empathy exist? Novels like Peter Heller's *The Dog Stars* (2012) show grief and compassion but, as I demonstrate in Chapter 4, the juxtaposition of morality and materiality is complicated by a different kind of asymmetry relating to cannibal and consumed, survival and death. In part by exploring the multifaceted, relational, and differentiated ways in which cannibalism functions at points of privation and human extinction, I show how these novels interrogate faulty ideas about human exceptionalism and species difference.

The comfortable distinction between human beings and environments is challenged by scholars who work across disciplinary boundaries, and their

---

[59] Robert Redfield, *Human Nature and the Study of Society: The Papers of Robert Redfield*, ed. Margaret P. Redfield (Chicago, IL: Chicago University Press, 1962), quoted in Steven Lukes, *Moral Relativism* (London: Picador, 2008), 38.

conceptualizations help me articulate the breakdown of separations between humans, nonhumans, and the effects of ecocollapse in the chapters that follow. Karen Barad's theory of agential realism offers a crucial lens through which to consider practices of human exceptionalism; she urges an accounting "of the entangled materializations of which we are a part."[60] Her work focuses attention on the embeddedness of human bodies in the larger environment, the vast web of changing intra-actions that compose reality and "entail an ethical obligation to intra-act responsibly in the world's becoming, to contest and rework what matters and what is excluded from mattering" (178), and puts humans back into "the world-body space in its dynamic structuration" (185). The environment is no "blank slate" upon which humans enact their lives but is inextricably interconnected within and throughout, as Stacy Alaimo shows in her account of "trans-corporeality" in *Bodily Natures*.[61] Alaimo's robust cultural studies analysis of materiality breaks down otherwise rigid, bounded concepts of human agency to show how material interchanges and agency enfold as both environment and matter, "in which everything presumed to be outside of the properly human is always already within."[62] Cannibalism manifests additional levels of depth and complexity to interconnected notions of material incorporation and "bodily nature."

Chapter Summaries

Ecocollapse Fiction and Cultures of Human Extinction continues with Chapter 2, which counteracts the commitment to absolute individual subjectivity that weaves through much climate change fiction by launching with Yann Martel's *Life of Pi*, a novel described by Louise Westling as revealing "a desperate struggle whose stark essentials may become our future."[63] *Life of*

---

[60]   Karen Barad, *Meeting the Universe Halfway: Quantum Physics and the Entanglement of Matter and Meaning* (Durham, NC: Duke University Press, 2007), 384. Subsequent citations appear parenthetically in the text.

[61]   And in Alaimo's other works, including *Material Feminisms*, edited with Susan J. Hekman (Bloomington: Indiana University Press, 2007).

[62]   Stacy Alaimo, *Bodily Natures: Science, Environment, and the Material Self* (Bloomington: Indiana University Press, 2010), 155.

[63]   Louise Westling, *The Logos of the Living World: Merleau-Ponty, Animals, and Language* (New York: Fordham University Press, 2014), 134.

Pi's multiplicitious collisions, overlaps, and intersections of embedded agencies enable valuable considerations of complex human and nonhuman materiality interwoven in shared, ecocollapsed worldspaces. I argue that the novel undermines hierarchical proclivities that haunt the anthropocentric subject and demonstrate how, by imagining a shipwrecked, castaway experience as a vastly curtailed ecological world, it envisions catastrophic climate change and the entangled-and-untangleable intricacies that reject the impulse of human exceptionalism and defensive individualism. In *Life of Pi*, the human becomes extinct as a unified subject independent of the rest of the environment's agencies, but even though Pi's "I" collapses, *Life of Pi* provides an escape from the lifeboat, so the next chapter explores what happens when there is no refuge from ecocollapse and literal species extinction.

Chapter 3 analyzes the unlivable global ecosystems and devastated personal landscapes in Helen Simpson's "Diary of an Interesting Year" and Cormac McCarthy's *The Road* to explore their obliterations of human exceptionalism, moral codes, bodily integrity, and the concomitant reframing of ethical, social, and species boundaries amid the two stages of human extinction events they describe. Rejecting the kind of attachment articulated in Lauren Berlant's *Cruel Optimism*, the "Diary" narrator refuses the vulnerability seen in *The Road*'s father figure's desperate dependence on his child's survival as motivation to construct an ongoing "life." The man in *The Road* defines his cruelly optimistic morality in opposition to the cannibals he fears are all around them, but I show how that righteousness is in fact slippery (they are themselves "cannibals" by their own definitions) and the supposed cannibals further interweave agencies of becoming in the ecocollapsed world. The feminist reframing of vulnerability in "Diary" and the enculturation of cannibalism in *The Road* incorporate epistemological ruptures that dissolve notions of human exceptionalism, so rather than redemptive or hopeful endings, there is no meaningful *life* to survive for; rather, these ecocollapse fictions imagine the struggle for agential *death*.

Chapter 4 brings these intersections into confrontation by interrogating climate change, disease, and the disintegration of humanity in Peter Heller's *The Dog Stars*, as problematized alongside the worldviews uncovered in *The Road*, "Diary," and *Life of Pi*, and contrasted to another post-pandemic scenario fictionalized in Emily St. John Mandel's *Station Eleven* (2014), which has a happy ending and therefore perpetuates the "hopeful future" genre. I argue that Heller's novel explores grief, agency, and compassion while the narrator documents the human species going extinct, individual by individual, in a rapidly warming world, acknowledging the truth as the last survivor that "life and death lived inside each other."[64] The juxtaposition of morality and materiality is complicated by a different kind of asymmetry relating to cannibal and consumed, survival and death here. My analysis demonstrates that extant primitivist utopias do not continue by the end of the novel (in contrast to the work of other scholars, who interpret the conclusion optimistically), despite what superficially appears to be a remaining community of survivors. This chapter illustrates that, as in the other fictions of ecocollapse examined here, the human species in *The Dog Stars* cannot regenerate. The narrator is the last human survivor.

Chapter 5 advances human species' membership as part of an active landscape of processes, human and nonhuman, political, cultural, environmental, racialized, and gendered, in constant interchange, with uneven distributions of risk and harm. Rather than the apathy, disempowerment, and skepticism shown to be produced by fear-inducing media coverage of climate change or false hope as in post-apocalyptic climate fiction's popular generic conventions, this chapter argues that realistic examples of ecocollapse and human extinction have the capacity to help readers imagine beyond the vague notion of "species extinction" and toward an acceptance of death itself that can raise evocative potential. While textual explorations in previous chapters explicated the characters' adaptive responses as mortal animals no longer deluded by human exceptionalism in ecocollapsed worlds, this chapter valuably directs the focus of analysis toward issues of justice and injustice, various structural inequalities, and the systemic oppressions at work in these novels. I unpack the damaging repercussions of colonialism, global inequality, racism, poverty, and other sociopolitical marginalizations that contribute to differentiated types of vulnerability in the Anthropocene. I show how the subtlety of these fictions' extinctions and the deferment of the last death helps frame readers' adaptations to changing environments with acceptance that these extinction events are happening and might happen

---

[64]   Peter Heller, *The Dog Stars* (New York: Vintage Books, 2012), 68.

to us individually. "We read," Tobias Menely and Jesse Oak Taylor observe, "because we are terrified. We read to confront our complicity, to ratify our guilt, to mourn our losses,"[65] and it is the creative writer's responsibility, according to Bill McKibben, "to help us understand what things feel like."[66] I argue that human extinction is the ultimate dismantling of alluring belief systems rooted in human exceptionalism. Acceptance can lead to peace with the notion of change and the impermanence of all things, which might lead to space for compassion, empathy, and action without fear. Finally, by responding to Haraway's appeal toward taking "pleasure in the confusion of boundaries and the responsibility in their construction,"[67] I also account for the ways that extinction plays a significant role in the potential flourishing of other life-forms as a final rejection of human exceptionalism: this is, after all, the *sixth* great extinction. What might evolve into the new ecosystems of climate-changed earth?

---

[65] Tobias Menely and Jesse Oak Taylor, introduction to *Anthropocene Reading: Literary History in Geologic Times*, eds. Tobias Menely and Jesse Oak Taylor (University Park: Pennsylvania State University, 2017), 20.

[66] Bill McKibben, introduction to *I'm with the Bears: Short Stories from a Damaged Planet*, ed. Mark Martin (New York: Verso, 2011), 3.

[67] Although I do not mean this in a technoscience way. See Donna Haraway, "A Cyborg Manifesto," in *Simians, Cyborgs and Women: The Reinvention of Nature* (New York: Routledge, 1991), 150.

2

Irreducible Entanglement: "All Was Kith and Kin" in *Life of Pi*

Yann Martel's *Life of Pi* is a story that undermines hierarchical proclivities and provides an occasion for rethinking human exceptionalism in vastly diminished ecosystems while it avoids generating new universalisms that risk making invisible how precarity falls most heavily on vulnerable populations. The human exceptionalism that haunts climate change denial cannot survive the destruction of its own categories of difference. Although on the surface the novel is about an adolescent Indian boy cast adrift in a lifeboat with a 450-pound Bengal tiger, it is really a complex demonstration of the limitations of the very binaries created to categorize human entitlements. The novel unifies a long list of oppositions: human/nonhuman, animal/vegetable, wild/civilized, cannibal/vegetarian, science/religion, fact/fiction, freedom/security, and self/other, to name just a few, demonstrating that the web of the world is reciprocally engaged, agential, and interconnected. The nonhuman world is a verb, not a noun: in Pi's words describing an epiphanic moment, "Tree took account of road, which was aware of air, which was mindful of sea, which shared things with sun. Every element lived in harmonious relation with its neighbour, and all was kith and kin."[1] By also imagining a shipwrecked, castaway experience as a greatly diminished ecological world, the novel envisions catastrophic climate change, individual trauma, and the necessity of vital connections to others, place, and multispecies social worlds. My argument here is that *Life of Pi* can show us how we might reject the impulse of human exceptionalism

---

[1] Yann Martel, *Life of Pi: A Novel* (Orlando, FL: Harcourt, 2001), 62. Subsequent citations appear parenthetically in the text.

that pervades Western thought as we encounter climate change and ecological collapse, by attending to the novel's flattening of hierarchies that separate the human from the rest of the natural world and intertwining of everything into an interconnected, entangled-and-untangleable intricacy.

This approach to the novel emphasizes its imbrication of human action and nonhuman agency, following Karen Barad and Donna Haraway, that we might begin by exploring the title character's integration of a complex human identity into a world of ecological solidarity. Like Schrodinger's cat, Pi is indeterminate, and his name is simultaneously specific and infinite, unifying disparate entities and concepts into a sort of cohesive harmony. Mr. Patel reveals that his given name, Piscine Molitor Patel, is inspired by a swimming pool so beloved by family friend Mamaji that his parents named him after "the crowning aquatic glory of . . . the entire civilized world" despite being unable to swim themselves (11). Mamaji so loves the aquatic complex that words fail him, illustrating language's inability to articulate the multifacetedness that is Pi (or *anything* in a phenomenological world). "It was a pool the gods would have delighted to swim in," Mamaji begins:

> "There were two pools, an indoor and an outdoor. Both were as big as small oceans. . . . The water was so clean and clear you could have used it to make your morning coffee. Wooden changing cabins, blue and white, surrounded the pool on two floors. You could look down and see everyone and everything. . . . The showers gushed hot, soothing water. There was a steam room and an exercise room. The outside pool became a skating rink in winter. There was a bar, a cafeteria, a large sunning deck, even two small beaches with real sand. Every bit of tile, brass and wood gleamed. It was—it was . . ."

> It was the only pool that made Mamaji fall silent. (11–12)

The Piscine Molitor was a full recreational complex known for its art deco resemblance to an ocean liner that housed fashion shows and theater performances: it slipped between many ways of being just like Pi, who is both the water and the boy in it, both the ship and the shipwrecked, both a boy and a tiger, becomes many ways of being concurrently.

Piscine's chosen nickname, Pi, is equally remarkable as "that elusive, irrational number with which scientists try to understand the universe" (24).

On his first day at secondary school in Pondicherry, Piscine renames himself to escape the teasing catcalls of "Pissing" by his classmates (Piscine Molitor's water imagery includes human water as well as pool and ocean water). When attendance is taken in each class, Pi boldly marks on the chalkboards "My name is Piscine Molitor Patel, known to all as Pi Patel π = 3.14," drawing a large circle "sliced into with a diameter, to evoke the basic lesson of geometry" (23). By including the symbol, π, Pi correlates himself with mathematical concepts that cannot be fully comprehended nor expressed by language: infinity, irrationality, and transcendence. Through the symbol, Pi encompasses a concept that unites the infinite (the number in its entirety) and the finite (the representation of that entirety) and takes refuge "in that Greek letter that looks like a shack with a corrugated tin roof" (24).[2] Connecting himself to the mysterious power that threatens human existence in the book of Exodus, Pi orders food under the name "I am who I am,"[3] which the pizzeria employee mishears as Ian Hoolihan. The various ways that Pi makes meaning of and redefines his name echoes Barad's contention that "The knowing subject is enmeshed in a thick web of representations such that the mind cannot see its way to objects that are now forever out of reach and all that is visible is the sticky problem of humanity's own captivity within language."[4] Nothing is immutable.

True to Pi's claim that "telling about something [is] already something of an invention" (302), it is nearly impossible to impose a linear structure onto the novel because the plot itself demonstrates the very undecidability and simultaneity that a breakdown of human exceptionalism demands. It weaves in and out of realities and can only be fully appreciated after reading it through and then reassessing from the beginning to apprehend the newly deeper significance of each prose line (as further demonstration of the novel's genius, it thus fulfills Pi's own wish for "a long book with a never-ending story"

---

[2] Additionally, "Pi" is a homophone with the circular, bisected baked pastry. When Piscine's brother Ravi indicates approval of Pi's new nickname, he says, "Anything's better than 'Pissing'. Even 'Lemon Pie'" (24).

[3] Exodus 3:13–14: But Moses said to God, "If I come to the Israelites and say to them, 'The God of your ancestors has sent me to you', and they ask me, 'What is his name?' what shall I say to them?" God said to Moses, "I am who I am." *The New Oxford Annotated Bible*, ed. Michael D. Coogan, 3rd ed. (Oxford: Oxford University Press, 2001), 87.

[4] Karen Barad, "Posthumanist Performativity: Toward an Understanding of How Matter Comes to Matter," *Signs: Journal of Women in Culture and Society* 28, no. 3 (2003): 811–12.

[207]). Although *Life of Pi* begins with a fictional "Author's Note," there is also a beginning that recalls folktales from childhood: "Once upon a time there was a zoo in the Pondicherry Botanical Garden" (xi). From his adult perspective, Pi recalls his college studies at the University of Toronto, his childhood in India as the son of a zookeeper, the intertwining of his religious faiths, and the events when he was cast adrift on a lifeboat with a tiger, a hyena, a wounded zebra, an orangutan, a rat, flies, and eleven cockroaches after the ship they were sailing to Toronto sinks in the middle of the Pacific Ocean. It is a wrenching account of hunger, loss, and love as the young vegetarian boy witnesses the injured zebra and orangutan attacked and consumed by the hyena, who is then killed and eaten by the tiger in an intimate display of ferocity on a tiny lifeboat, where Pi and the tiger, misnamed Richard Parker as a cub, survive more than seven months at sea before finally landing ashore in Mexico. There, Pi is interviewed by investigators whose incredulity about his first story persuades him to tell another that replaces the animals with humans, turning interspecies companionship into murder, cannibalism, and isolation. Finally, he shares a third plausible story, devoid of details. Each version of his experience, however, demonstrates that "all living things contain a measure of madness that moves them in strange, sometimes inexplicable ways. This madness can be saving; it is part and parcel of the ability to adapt. Without it, no species would survive" (41). The animal other is indistinguishable from the human self; science and religion, truth and fiction, vegetarian and carnivore, animal and plant, all weave and wind together until finally everything converges. Consequently, the novel's heterogeneous defiance of boundaries becomes an experimentation that destabilizes lifeboat narrative conventions and creates space for reconsidering ecocollapse.

We first see this syncretization when the adult Pi begins telling his story, describing the three-toed sloths about whose thyroid function he wrote his undergraduate thesis at the University of Toronto. Although Pi states that he "chose the sloth because its demeanour—calm, quiet, and introspective—did something to soothe [his] shattered self" (3), the sloth also exactly models the uniting of animal and plant life in a peaceful organism that lives "in perfect harmony with its environment" (4). Sloths are vegetarian and spend most of their sedentary days hanging from tree limbs in rain forests of South and Central America, camouflaged by the various plants and animals that take up residence in their fur. They have deeply symbiotic relationships with bacteria (without whom they cannot digest their food), and their feces provide nutrients for the trees whose leaves they consume.[5] Furthermore, as Pi says, "A sloth's hairs shelter an algae that is brown during the dry season and green during the wet season, so the animal blends in with the surrounding moss and foliage and looks like a nest of white ants or of squirrels, or like nothing at all but part of a tree" (4). Sloths also host small moths and beetles in their fur, becoming one with the landscape as a vivid place where plant, animal, and insect meet and mingle in valuable, entangled material life. In fact, "Such a miracle of life reminded [Pi] of God" (5).

But which God? Here too, everything is entangled. The sloths remind Pi of "upside-down yogis deep in mediation or hermits deep in prayer, wise beings whose intense imaginative lives were beyond the reach of my scientific probing" (5). In other words, even this question has no simple answer because Pi demonstrates interconnectivity and cohesive harmony by desiring to love God as a devout Hindu, Christian, and Muslim simultaneously. He figures that "Hindus, in their capacity for love, are indeed hairless Christians, just as Muslims, in the way they see God in everything, are bearded Hindus, and Christians, in their devotion to God, are hat-wearing Muslims" (50). Arrogant religious elitism is signified by the three faiths' leaders who insist that Pi must choose. As Karla Suomala argues in her essay about interfaith dialogue, strict religious separation occurs because "conceptions of religious identity, both in academia and in the pew, are largely based on these older institutional models of identity and affiliation and reflect the same fears toward mixture and change."[6] Pi's complex religious identity flattens hierarchical compartmentalizations into a horizontal triangle bounded by love, devotion, and universality: even religious exceptionalism is rejected. This triangle is replicated in the three hills in Munnar upon which stood three Godhouses and the three stories Mr. Patel tells of his religious development. Through his concomitant beliefs, Pi can comprehend the universe wholly as divine, refusing to give more than names to the concepts beyond human understanding:

---

[5] See Alina Bradford, "Sloths: The World's Slowest Mammals," *Live Science*, November 26, 2018, https://www.livescience.com/27612-sloths.html.

[6] Karla Suomala, "Complex Religious Identity in the Context of Interfaith Dialogue," *Crosscurrents: The Association for Religion and Intellectual Life* 62, no. 3 (September 2012): 364.

> There is Brahman, the world soul, the sustaining frame upon which is woven, warp and weft, the cloth of being, with all its decorative elements of space and time. There is Brahman nirguna, without qualities, which lies beyond understanding, beyond description, beyond approach; with our poor words we sew a suit for it . . . and try to make it fit, but Brahman nirvana always bursts the seams. We are left speechless. (48)

From his Christian teacher he learns humanity and love; from his Muslim teacher, brotherhood and devotion, but ultimately he learns all from each. Throughout his lifeboat ordeal, he calls on all faiths to sustain him, entangling seemingly opposing conceptualizations of "God" into one flesh: his own. There is no way to preserve the distinctiveness of individual religious doctrines that on their face are mutually incompatible but function in unity as Pi's complex religious identity. He troubles the impulse to cultivate cultural or religious privilege by prioritizing divinity over the particularities of variously constructed faiths. To put it another way: it is only from a singular perspective that the sloth is hanging "upside down."

In addition to syncretizing religions, Pi further combats hierarchical, exceptionalistic thinking with the limitations of language by richly entwining religious studies and zoology, noting that "The obsession with putting ourselves at the centre of everything is the bane not only of theologians but also of zoologists" (31). At the University of Toronto, he double-majored in religious studies and zoology, writing one undergraduate thesis about cosmogony theory and another about the three-toed sloths—faith versus science, a binary opposition he unifies throughout the novel. The sloths' meditations lie beyond the reach of his scientific questioning and "That which sustains the universe beyond thought and language, and that which is at the core of us and struggles for expression, is the same thing. The finite within the infinite, the infinite within the finite" (48–9) even as it evades his linguistic efforts to represent that entanglement in words. Similarly, two of Pi's beloved teachers, Mr. Kumar the Communist biology teacher and Mr. Kumar the Sufi baker, superficially share nothing in common except their name, which Martel uses to twist them into one: "Mr. and Mr. Kumar taught me biology and Islam. Mr. and Mr. Kumar led me to study zoology and religious studies at the University of Toronto. Mr. and Mr. Kumar were the prophets of my youth" (61). When the Mr. Kumars meet each other in front of the zebra enclosure at the zoo, the passage no longer describes them as separate men. Who is whom matters no more than whether a zebra is white with black stripes or vice versa.

The novel exposes the way that boundaries between humans and animals are constructed and trespassed as well, most extensively in the relationship between Pi and the tiger Richard Parker. Richard Parker is first mentioned in the context of Pi's reminiscences, although at this point readers assume that he is human, so his subjective experience of the world is perplexing:

> Richard Parker has stayed with me. I've never forgotten him. Dare I say I miss him? I do. I miss him. I still see him in my dreams. They are nightmares mostly, but nightmares tinged with love. Such is the strangeness of the human heart. I still cannot understand how he could abandon me so unceremoniously, without any sort of goodbye, without looking back even once. That pain is like an axe that chops at my heart. (6)

Because there is no indication that Richard Parker is a tiger at this point in the novel, his refusal to give a parting sendoff must be reexamined pages later when it becomes clear he is not human. The obfuscation of Richard Parker's tigerness can also be scrutinized through the lens of his naming: "Richard Parker was so named because of a clerical error" (132), "clerical" meaning secretarial (associated with an office) and religious (associated with a church). The tiger cub is both: he is baptized "Thirsty" by the hunter who kills his mother and is documented on official paperwork as "Richard Parker" and the hunter's name as "Thirsty None Given" (133). The switching of names insinuates that the practice of naming humans is a laughable one of arbitrary categorization. However, despite his name, Richard Parker remains a tiger in the novel and does not take on any of the wishful, anthropomorphic characteristics Pi himself describes of zoo visitors, who construct "*Animalus anthropomorphicus*, the animal as seen through human eyes" (31). Instead, the tiger is really and truly a tiger, exhibiting Haraway's conception of nonhuman response (as contrasted with mere reaction) in the ethics described in *The Companion Species Manifesto*. Even though Pi wishes Richard Parker would acknowledge their shared experience with a proper goodbye, he knows that desire is part of the human obsession to "put ourselves at the center of everything" (31), which he resists.

Readers have to struggle against the desire to put the human at the center of our interpretations of this novel, too, so Martel insures that Richard Parker's agency butts up against both Pi's fragile animal body and any predetermined expectations of human exceptionalism readers may have. For example, although Pi lists seven ways in which he might survive the shipwreck and chooses Plan Number Seven, the only one that does not involve some plot to kill the tiger,[7] Richard Parker influences the decision in the first place with his calm acceptance of Pi (perhaps his own Plan Number Seven?):

> It was Richard Parker who calmed me down. It is the irony of this story that the one who scared me witless to start with was the very same who brought me peace, purpose, I dare say even wholeness.
>
> He was looking at me intently. After a time I recognized the gaze. I had grown up with it. It was the gaze of a contented animal. . . . He was simply taking me in, observing me, in a manner that was sobering but not menacing. He kept twitching his ears and varying the sideways turn of his head. . . .
>
> He made a sound, a snort from his nostrils. I pricked up my ears. He did it a second time. I was astonished. Prusten? (162–3)

Prusten, Pi explains, is the quietest tiger call and expresses friendliness and harmless intentions, and here maps a blurring of species boundaries via communicative language, the very thing Aristotle first erected as a criterion for moral value that excluded nonhuman animals. "Richard Parker did it again, this time with a rolling of the head. He looked exactly as if he were asking me a question" (164). Their reciprocal gaze is suggestive of an agreement toward mutual care that destabilizes the typical ecocastrophe narrative structure. Janet Fiskio, drawing on the work of Garrett Hardin and Rebecca Solnit, identifies two dominant narratives in climate change discourse: what she calls the "lifeboat," wherein "the neoclassical economic view of humans as rational agents who make choices to further their self-interest prevails," and the "collective," which "offers the possibility of creating new modes of politics and new communities."[8] Rather than one or the other of these, *Life of Pi* is a lifeboat collective because,

---

[7] The other plans to get rid of Richard Parker are, One: Push him off the lifeboat; Two: Kill him with six morphine syringes; Three: Attack him with all available weaponry; Four: Choke him; Five: Poison him, set him on fire, electrocute him; Six: Wage a war of attrition. See 157–8.

[8] Janet Fiskio, "Apocalypse and Ecotopia: Narratives in Global Climate Change Discourse," *Race, Gender & Class* 19, nos. 1–2 (2012): 14.

by exchanging a mutual gaze, Pi and Richard Parker acknowledge each other's subjectivity, each other's presence in the same space as agents-in-the-world. Their gaze is one of reciprocal participatory recognition.

Ethical reciprocity in which we make ourselves open to responsiveness invokes John Berger's influential essay "Why Look at Animals?" in which he claims that modern industrial societies have extinguished the possibility of shared looks between humans and other animals by imprisoning animals' bodies within the degrading walls of zoo enclosures and otherwise transforming their images into spectacles.[9] In Berger's view, even companion animals like dogs cannot exchange a gaze with their humans because "they have been co-opted into the family" and "in this relationship the autonomy of both parties has been lost."[10] Perhaps as a critique of anthropocentric claims like these, Jacques Derrida describes how his kitten challenges his ability to convey the actuality of his existence via her disorienting gaze.[11] His naked body's exposure triggers a malaise brought upon by his inarticulate recognition of the limits of his subjectivity—the "who am I at this moment" question he later calls the "abyssal limit of the human."[12] The cat's gaze—her subjectivity—becomes a mirror to reflect Derrida's own humanness, represented by his shame and nakedness. In other words, the cat's gaze represents "the point of view of the absolute other."[13] Similarly for Martin Buber some sixty years earlier, dialogue with a cat demonstrates *I-Thou* relations: "the beginning of this cat's glance, lighting up under the touch of my glance, indisputably questioned me: 'Is it possible that you think of me? . . . Do I concern you? Do I exist in your sight? Do I really exist? What is it that comes from you? What is it that surrounds me? What is it that comes to me? What is it?' "[14] His encounter with the gaze

---

[9] John Berger, "Why Look at Animals?" in *About Looking* (New York: Vintage Books, 1980), 3–28.

[10] Ibid., 15.

[11] Susan Fraiman's astute critique of Derrida's troubling gender politics and her convincing arguments about the shortcomings of the following passages are worth noting here, although she moves beyond the scope of my specific point regarding the gaze. Fraiman problematizes this scene to demonstrate that "Derrida's cat is granted provisional subject status in implicitly humanist terms—ones that continue to reflect the premium placed by our own upright species on the 'higher' faculties" (96). See Fraiman, "Pussy Panic versus Liking Animals: Tracking Gender in Animal Studies," *Critical Inquiry* 39 (Autumn 2012): 89–115.

[12] Jacques Derrida, "The Animal That Therefore I Am (More to Follow)," in *The Animal That Therefore I Am*, ed. Marie-Louise Mallet, trans. David Wills (New York: Fordham University Press, 2008), 3, 12.

[13] Ibid., 11.

[14] Martin Buber, *I and Thou* (New York: Scribner, 1958), 97.

of another animal thus disputes several traditional philosophical assumptions about the limits of nonhuman subjectivity, contending instead that other animals can look, that animality in general does not exist, and that even this cat, who is "family" and familiar (in Berger's terms), can call into question his construction of self (à la Levinas) and expand it into *I-Thou* relations in the Buberian sense. Accordingly, these philosophers help us elucidate what Pi struggles to communicate about his experience with Richard Parker and his soft vocalization. Both animals make a choice in the passage where Pi hears "prusten": both the human and the tiger decide that they will live or die together, and they choose mutual care. Thus, while we read Pi's internal decision-making process by which he selects Plan Number Seven, we witness Richard Parker's communicative agency and the effect it produces in Pi after they exchange a disorienting gaze.

Similarly, although Pi coaches Richard Parker to respect his territory on the lifeboat, Richard Parker also trains Pi to read his signals: they are two species communicating across the abyss. The tiger can kill and eat the boy at any time but does not, although he swipes at him repeatedly during their mutual efforts as they strive to understand each other's languages. As Pi states, "If I survived my apprenticeship as a high seas animal trainer, it was because Richard Parker did not really want to attack me" (206). Instead of deadly assaults from both sides, they teach each other: Pi whistles and rocks the lifeboat to communicate and Richard Parker cuffs him, knocking Pi into the sea until

> Eventually I learned to read the signals he was sending me. I found that with his ears, his eyes, his whiskers, his teeth, his tail and his throat, he spoke a simple, forcefully punctuated language that told me what his next move might be. I learned to back down before he lifted his paw in the air. Then I made my point, feet on the gunnel, boat rolling, my single-note language blasting from the whistle, and Richard Parker moaning and gasping at the bottom of the boat. (207)

Both imagine the experience and perspective of the other to avoid a dangerous confrontation, one which would leave the victor even more vulnerable to near-certain death. They reciprocate a kind of mutual care. In this way, two disparate creatures manage to shepherd each other toward survival.

Also, although some critics[15] have labeled Pi the tiger's "master" (and Pi himself uses this term), the text reveals that he is more rightly called Richard Parker's "steward" and vice versa: human exceptionalism has no place in the barely sustainable ecosystem, and human and tiger are equally attentive and receptive. For example, Pi fills up the tiger's bucket with fresh water and gives him "the lion's share" of whatever food is caught (224) while also respecting his territorial need for space and his comfort at the bottom of the boat under the tarp. The traditional human/animal hierarchy is overturned when the boy privileges the tiger's psychological and material needs over his own physical requirements. Correspondingly, Richard Parker respects Pi's territory above the tarp, does not assert his greater physical strength, and provides Pi with companionship, motivation, and purpose. As Pi says, "If he died I would be alone with despair, a foe even more formidable than a tiger. If I still had a will to live, it was thanks to Richard Parker. He kept me from thinking too much about my family and my tragic circumstances. He pushed me to go on living" (164). Neither can survive without the other: Richard Parker offers Pi an escape from despair while Pi is a physical provider for Richard Parker (and, for all we know, is a psychological comfort to him as well). Thus, firm divisions between domination and submission become complicated by their shared, entangled needs. When Pi tries to claim a superior "human" status rather than acknowledge that he is "the very definition of an animal" too, by insisting that he is "a human being," Richard Parker (maybe) reestablishes mutuality, responding aloud: "What boastful pride" (247). Pi, blind at the time, does not know who is actually speaking here. It may be Richard Parker; it may be another castaway, also blind, encountered in the middle of the Pacific; it may be himself; it may be the Cook: all potentialities are entangled until the reader decides which is most convincing. As Barad illustrates in her rethinking of quantum physics, it is the observer—the reader—who influences the interpretative outcome.

Pi's entanglement with Richard Parker helps explain his consternation when the tiger refuses to acknowledge Pi when they finally land on the beach in Mexico, modeling one of the challenges of conceptualizing the interior

---

[15] For example, Phillip Armstrong, Rebecca Duncan, Jane Elliot, and others.

processes of any other being.[16] After he leaps onto the beach, the tiger denies Pi the final anthropomorphic moment—the tearful goodbye—reinforcing his animal agency once again in case readers have fallen into romanticized idealizations like Pi suddenly cannot resist doing:

> He didn't look at me. He ran a hundred yards or so along the shore before turning in. His gait was clumsy and uncoordinated. He fell several times. At the edge of the jungle, he stopped. I was certain he would turn my way. He would look at me. He would flatten his ears. He would growl. In some such way, he could conclude our relationship. He did nothing of the sort. He only looked fixedly into the jungle. Then Richard Parker, companion of my torment, awful, fierce thing that kept me alive, moved forward and disappeared forever from my life. (284–5)

Thus, the novel deconstructs the desire to center humans and enables the tiger to maintain his tigerness throughout while acknowledging Pi's very human wish for a conclusive ending to their relationship. However, Richard Parker's immediate escape from the lifeboat into the jungle is also a comment about freedom being important for all animals, not just humans. The boat restricts the tiger in much the same way as the zoo described in the early sections of the novel, so Richard Parker's departure challenges what appears to be Pi's justification of zoos.

Early chapters of *Life of Pi* include what appears to be a robust defense of zoo practices. The Pondicherry Botanical Garden's zoo is described as a "huge zoo, spread over numberless acres, big enough to require a train to explore it" (12). Part of a garden, there is a "riot of flowers" everywhere, and "suddenly, amidst the tall and slim trees up ahead, you notice two giraffes quietly observing you. The sight is not the last of your surprises. The next moment you are startled by a furious outburst coming from a great troupe of monkeys, only outdone in volume by the shrill cries of strange birds" (12, 13). There are no visible barriers; instead, suddenly giraffes or monkeys or rhinoceros come into view and are described as the ones with the power to gaze, "quietly observing you" (13). Leisurely visitors sit on benches and enjoy the sights and sounds of the human and nonhuman animals around them, both noticing and being noticed.

---

[16]   See Thomas Nagel's "What Is It Like to Be a Bat?" *Philosophical Review* 83, no. 4 (October 1974): 435–50.

According to Pi, the zoo's captive animals are relaxed and content (if not even pleased) in their respective spaces because "In a zoo, we do for animals what we have done for ourselves with houses: we bring together in a small space what in the wild is spread out. . . . An animal will take possession of its zoo space in the same way it would lay claim to a new space in the wild, exploring it and marking it out in the normal ways of its species, with sprays of urine perhaps" (17, 18). Pi says that the animals' total dependence on humans for their needs is preferable to the perils of the wild. This perspective stands in direct contrast to Randy Malamud's observation that a zoo exhibit "really offers little insight into the natural condition of that species" because of that very dependence and concludes that the only outcome is the substantiation of human superiority.[17] The paradox of zoo animals is clear: the natural within the cultural, they are neither wild nor domesticated. More accurately, zoo inhabitants have the status of exiled refugees, according to Bob Mullan and Garry Marvin: "Denied access to their natural habitat these animals become marginalized from their wild nature and begin to lose access to the mentalities and behaviors which would have been appropriate there. Such animals have a status akin to that of refugees. They are in enforced exile, but a false one at that, because realistically there is no 'home' to return to."[18] Pi argues instead that the greatest harm to the zoo animals is the ignorant people who come to look at them, saying "our species' excessive predatoriness has made the entire planet our prey. More specifically, we have in mind the people who feed fishhooks to the otters, razors to the bears, apples with small nails in them to the elephants and hardware variations on the theme . . . The cruelty is often more active and direct," he continues (29), giving a long list of various harms the visitors have inflicted on the creatures inhabiting the zoo to conclude that the most dangerous animal in the Pondicherry Botanical Garden is the human animal.

Nonetheless, Pi's apparent defense of zoos is a controversial issue among the community of scholars interested in challenging the objectification of nonhuman life. For example, Philip Armstrong contends that Pi's defense of zoo practices and the concomitant disregard for the lives of real animals'

[17]   Randy Malamud, *Reading Zoos: Representations of Animals and Captivity* (New York: New York University Press, 1998), 1, 2.
[18]   Robert Mullan and Gary Marvin, *Zoo Culture: The Book about Watching People Watch Animals*, 2nd ed. (Urbana: University of Illinois Press, 1998), 29.

suffering in real zoos marks this novel as one that "presents humans as innately different from and superior to animals because they possess a greater capacity for rational inventiveness, adaptability to new circumstances, and mobility."[19] Superficially, Armstrong's claims appear to be the case. Pi notes that predation, danger, hunger, thirst, parasites, and fear mean that animals are never really free in the wild, regardless of environmentalists' protests to the contrary: "Animals in the wild lead lives of compulsion and necessity," he says, and are "free neither in space nor in time, nor in their personal relations" (16). And he would know, after existing on a lifeboat for seven months of "freedom." Pi puts it even more straightforwardly, though: "Think about it yourself. Would you rather be put up at the Ritz with free room service and unlimited access to a doctor or be homeless without a soul to care for you?" (18). But the answer to this question is much more complicated even for Pi, despite what appears to be his championing of zoo practices.

When it comes down to it, Pi does not believe his own claims about zoos. A week after the Tsimtsum sinks, Pi realizes that "with every passing day the lifeboat was resembling a zoo enclosure more and more: Richard Parker had his sheltered area for sleeping and resting, his food stash, his lookout and now his water hole" (188–9). Obviously, though, neither Pi nor Richard Parker would consider the lifeboat preferable to nearly any other living situation and it is only because of Pi's efforts to feed and hydrate Richard Parker that the tiger's territory on the lifeboat is any semblance of his enclosure back in the Pondicherry Botanical Gardens (or Pi's space on the lifeboat like his own house back in Pondicherry). He and Richard Parker share a common fate, just as we all do on earth. In fact, both tiger and boy leave the lifeboat at the first possible opportunity, paralleling the fantasy of interplanetary escape in science fiction. When the ocean currents bring their boat to a bright green floating algae island that Pi thinks is "a chimera, a play of the mind" after so many days at sea, he says, "In the near distance I saw trees. I did not react. I was certain it was an illusion that a few blinks would make disappear. . . . I blinked deliberately, expecting my eyelids to act like lumberjacks. But the trees did not fall" (256–7). The strange island, the fabric of which "seemed

[19]   Phillip Armstrong, *What Animals Mean in the Fiction of Modernity* (New York: Routledge, 2008), 178.

to be an intricate, tightly webbed mass of tube-shaped seaweed, in diameter a little thicker than two fingers" (257), produces fresh water in inner ponds, edible, sugary-sweet vegetation for Pi, and easily caught meerkats for Richard Parker. It is bliss. Pi ponders the mystery of why Richard Parker returns to the lifeboat each night, incorrectly concluding that he is "attached to his den" (265) there because Pi does not yet know that the island is carnivorous. Until he discovers that harrowing fact, he spends days "eating and drinking and bathing and observing the meerkats and walking and running and resting and growing stronger. My running became smooth and unselfconscious, a source of euphoria. My skin healed. My pains and aches left me. Put simply, I returned to life" (269). Similarly, Richard Parker is reinvigorated: "By dint of stuffing himself with meerkats, his weight went up, his fur began to glisten again, and he returned to his healthy look of old," even marking trees with his claws and roaring in search of a mate (272).[20] The island, like the Ritz hotel in Pi's zoo analogy, provides for all of their physical needs.

The island organism has a kind of sinister agency revealed by Pi's scientific explorations. Pi discovers it is about twenty miles in circumference[21] of blindingly green algae visually broken occasionally by trees whose "roots did not go their own independent way into the algae, but rather joined it, became it. Which meant that these trees either lived in a symbiotic relationship with the algae, in a giving-and-taking that was to their mutual advantage, or, simpler still, were an integral part of the algae" (271). The island is alive in more ways than one: to conserve water and expose less surface to the sun on bright days, the weave of tubular algae becomes dense and tight, pulling the island to an increased height; on overcast days, it loosens to spread out and reduces in height. But this phenomenon is not simply a response to the sun, careful readers realize: the "Gandhain" algae also slackens in heavy seas to absorb the force of waves. Is it possible for plants to be sentient? The island, really a free-floating organism, certainly seems to be, a conclusion buoyed by how it acquires energy and nutrition: it filters out salt to create freshwater ponds, consuming animals and fish that are then killed in the freshwater, pulled up

---

[20] For Pi's claim that the best indication of a perfect zoo environment is an animal who reproduces, see 40.

[21] Gleefully, I used π to figure the diameter is about 6.3 miles ($c/\pi = d$).

from the seawater below by a current it controls. Although the island algae feeds the meerkats during the day, one night Pi is awakened by their frightened chatter to witness the island *itself* feeding:

> The sky was cloudless and the moon full. The land was robbed of its colour. Everything glowed strangely in shades of black, grey and white. It was the pond. Silver shapes were moving in it, emerging from below and breaking the black surface of the water.
>
> Fish. Dead fish. They were floating up from deep down. The pond— remember, forty feet across—was filling up with all kinds of dead fish until its surface was no longer black but silver. And from the way the surface kept on being disturbed, it was evident that more dead fish were coming up. (276–7)

By the morning, all the fish and at least one large shark have disappeared, consumed by the island itself. Only after finding a complete set of human teeth wrapped in fruit-like accumulations of leaves in a tree does Pi figure it all out, the horrible realization dawning on him like knowledge did on Eve and Adam: the island is predatory and carnivorous.

For many readers, the island chapter is the point in the narrative where they can no longer suspend disbelief: an island made of algae that filters saltwater into freshwater, creates ponds that kill fish by the hundreds, supports a colony of swimming meerkats, and consumes a human entirely except thirty-two teeth, which remain wrapped in leaves like an owl pellet wraps fur and bones? It is, as Pi says, "an exceptional botanical discovery" (256). But strange things happen even outside of fictional worlds. For example, a mysterious floating island was spotted in the South Pacific by officers in New Zealand's Royal Navy in August 2012. Measuring 250 by 30 nautical miles, the island is described by Navy officer Lieutenant Tim Oscar as "the weirdest thing I've seen in 18 years at sea" and caused much consternation before being identified as pumice rock, probably the result of undersea volcanic eruptions.[22] Indeed, if such a large mass can go undetected in the age of Google Earth, what else might exist outside of our limited, human ways of knowing? And that is one of the novel's

---

[22] "Pumice Raft Bigger than Area of Israel," news.com.au, August 10, 2012, http://www.news.com.au/world/breaking-news/undersea-eruption-creates-pumic-raft/news-story/C2e7dd297df3546e605b0c72b4dc4a2f.

many accomplishments with its island, which Pi compares to the botanical impossibility of a 300-year-old bonsai tree: there are many things humans do not know about this world. Perhaps a carnivorous, predatory island is not so unbelievable after all.

More importantly for our understanding of the enmeshed complexities of *Life of Pi*, the island functions to expose the falsehood of Pi's claims that animals accept zoo enclosures or of the benefits of the Ritz over an independent existence, leading us to a richer, more ambitious understanding of what the novel accomplishes here relating to human exceptionalism, ecological scarcity, and generic "lifeboat" narrative conventions. The falsity of Pi's rationalization of zoos is exposed when Pi abandons his island Ritz, asking "How much loneliness [can be] endured? How much hopelessness taken on? And after all that, what of it? What to show for it? . . . How long does it take for a broken spirit to kill a body that has food, water and shelter?" (282). He prefers "to set off and perish in search of my own kind [rather] than to live a lonely half-life of physical comfort and spiritual death on this murderous island" (283). He leaves the following night after filling the boat with as much fresh water, dead fish, and meerkat meat as it will hold and awaiting Richard Parker's return, knowing that "to leave him would mean to kill him" (283). In other words, the zoo—perhaps metaphorically comparable to non-earth planetary colonies in futuristic science fiction—offers no greater purpose than mere survival and is inadequate for *any* animal. Accordingly, Pi himself escapes his zoo for the uncertainty of the open ocean, indicating that a life of compulsion and necessity is preferable to the dependent security of an enclosure, no matter how ideal. In this way, Pi also draws parallels between animals who escape from the zoo and his family, who escape from the uncertainty of India's political turmoil in the 1970s. "Animals that escape," Pi claims, "go from the known into the unknown—and if there is one thing an animal usually hates above all else, it is the unknown" (41). Likewise, humans are willing to "uproot and leave everything they've known for a great unknown beyond the horizon . . . in the hope of a better life" (77). All are "simply wild creatures seeking to fit in" (42). Besides Pi's relationship with Richard Parker, the island provides the most important syncretization of binary oppositions toward our understanding of how *Life of Pi* can provide us models for imagining climate change and ecological collapse, specifically here in terms of how all life requires something more than mere survival. Whatever our human species' future, freedom must be an integral part, even if, as we will see in the next chapter, it is freedom to die.

We can gather a further message in *Life of Pi*'s uncompromising position regarding humanity's relation to the rest of the living world: biodiversity is vital to the survival of all species, as seen in the critical juxtaposition of the island with human behavior and in Pi's comment that "our species' excessive predatoriness has made the entire planet our prey" (29). The island is sinister not just because of its predatory, carnivorous nature—Pi does the same thing to survive—but because it consumes utterly everything.[23] There is absolutely no biodiversity:

> The air of the place carried no flies, no butterflies, no bees, no insects of any kind. The trees sheltered no birds. The plains hid no rodents, no grubs, no worms, no snakes, no scorpions; they gave rise to no other trees, no shrubs, no grasses, no flowers. The ponds harbored no freshwater fish. The seashore teemed with no weeds, no crabs, no crayfish, no coral, no pebbles, no rocks. With the single, notable exception of the meerkats, there was not the least foreign matter on the island, organic or inorganic. It was nothing but shining green algae and shining green trees. (271)

By emphasizing the consequences of a habitable environment that is bereft of biodiversity, the island demonstrates the troubling consequences of what Stacy Alaimo identifies as reasoning based solely on meeting human requirements: "an ecology devoid of living creatures other than human beings" where "the lively world is reduced to the material for meeting 'needs.'"[24] The island can support human and nonhuman life, but apparently just a boy, a tiger, and meerkats. It is not a fully fleshed, entangled world, any more than a Mars colony is a solution to our current climate crisis.

---

[23] Curiously, Louise Squire's analysis of *Life of Pi* in terms of sustainability does not attend to the island, whose lack of biodiversity seems fitting support for her claims about subject horizons and Pi's juxtapositions in relation to ecological sustainability. See "Circles Unrounded: Sustainability, Subject and Necessity in Yann Martel's *Life of Pi*" in *Literature and Sustainability: Concept, Text and Culture*, ed. Adeline Johns-Putra, John Parham, and Louise Squire (Manchester: Manchester University Press, 2017), 228–45.

[24] Stacy Alaimo, "Sustainable This, Sustainable That: New Materialisms, Posthumanism and Unknown Futures," *PMLA* 127, no. 3 (2012): 562.

I alluded above that Pi and the island eat in the same fashion to survive: *Life of Pi* further challenges simple definitions of morality and immorality, especially as they relate to the prominent themes of hunger and eating. *In toto* the novel interweaves plants that eat flesh, flesh that eats plants, flesh that eats flesh, and plants that eat plants. In utter revision of Cartesian dualisms, it constructs multiple and varied complications to problematize simple, traditional equations: the meerkats are carnivores but not killers, the algae island is photosynthetic and predatory, the vegetarian boy cannibalizes human flesh, and a lion eats a cotton sari. Even the fictional Author's Note—the first words of the novel—begins, "This book was born as I was hungry" (vii). The text seems to construct a duality with the vegetarian Pi and the carnivore Richard Parker, but in fact there is a third option that demands sustained theoretical attention: the cannibalism that equates all flesh as same flesh. Is not all eating a kind of survival cannibalism, the consumption of another's materiality? Vegetarian Pi eats black gram dhal rice and sambar, vegetable korma, potato masala, and spicy lentil rasam: all once-living plants. When he discovers the emergency rations on the lifeboat after four days of being terrorized by the hyena and tiger and without water or food, he imagines "masala dosai with a coconut chutney—hmmmmm! Even better: oothappam! HMMMMM! Oh! I brought my hands to my mouth—IDLI!" (143). Instead, he finds cartons of Seven Oceans Standard Emergency Ration: fortified biscuits made with animal fat, which Pi wisely decides "the vegetarian part of me would simply pinch its nose and bear" rather than starve (143). Soon he is a murderer, cracking a fish's spine under a blanket (so he cannot see the eyes, perhaps, and risk engaging in a reciprocated gaze?) with tears running down his face: "I wept heartily over this poor little deceased soul. It was the first sentient being I had ever killed. I was now a killer. I was now as guilty as Cain. I was sixteen years old, a harmless boy, bookish and religious, and now I had blood on my hands. It's a terrible burden to carry. All sentient life is sacred. I never forget to include this fish in my prayers" (183).[25] Although Pi gives the first fish to Richard Parker, he soon devours whatever the sea provides. As he says, "It is

[25] Interestingly but beyond the scope of my argument here, Pi receives "cuts and bruises" all over his body from the flying fish, almost as a blood payment of sorts for the sacrifice this one fish makes. Pi likens the sharp fish to the arrows that pierced St. Sebastian, who is said to have been martyred twice. See Martel, *Life of Pi*, 181.

simple and brutal: a person can get used to anything, even to killing" (185), becoming the vegetarian predator himself in what Louise Westling argues is the breakdown of his "illusory efforts to live outside the bloody economy of carnivorous existence."[26] When he reaches the island, Pi eats the sweet outer layer of the tangled algae. That sweetness is the result of the island's carnivory, because plants produce sugar from their food sources, so carnivore/herbivore remains tangled and complicated.

Life of Pi weaves literal cannibalism into both the story with the animals and the story with humans, further and conclusively blurring the distinctions between them and between the ways that life sustains life. All death is equal in Pi's prayers for those who died and sustained his body, breaking down additional illusions of human exceptionalism. Jacques Derrida outlines human subjectivity as one dependent upon sacrifice of the nonhuman ("carno-phallogocentrism" is his term for the dominant model of the subject as speaking, virile, and carnivorous[27]) so as to define the animal as that which is eaten and the human as that which is not eaten. "The moral question," Derrida argues, "is thus not, nor has it ever been: should one eat or not eat, eat this and not that, the living or the nonliving, man or animal, but since *one must* eat in any case and since it is and tastes good to eat, and since there's no other definition of the good, *how* for goodness sake should one *eat well*?"[28] By identifying with the other, he answers. In *When Species Meet*, Haraway further contends that "There is no category that makes killing innocent; there is no category or strategy that removes one from killing."[29] Haraway objects to the logic of sacrifice that empowers only humans with the agency to respond to one another, thereby excluding animals from the category of beings who can be "murdered." They can only be "killed," and efforts to do so while avoiding deliberate cruelty are masked in the guise of how cruelty animalizes the human, damages the very humanity of the human. In contrast, Haraway invokes an antidote for the problem of making others killable in her feminist insight that

[26] Louise Westling, *The Logos of the Living World: Merleau-Ponty, Animals, and Language* (New York: Fordham University Press, 2014), 133.
[27] Jacques Derrida, "'Eating Well,' Or the Calculation of the Subject: An Interview with Jacques Derrida," in *Who Comes After the Subject?* ed. Eduardo Cadava, Peter Connor, and Jean-Luc Nancy (New York: Routledge, 1991), 113.
[28] Ibid., 115. Emphasis in original.
[29] Donna J. Haraway, *When Species Meet* (Minneapolis: University of Minnesota Press, 2008), 106.

a solution is for humans to kill responsibly *and be killed* responsibly, "yearning for the capacity to respond and to recognize response, always with reasons but knowing there will never be sufficient reason," to learn to kill well and die well, both.[30] *Life of Pi* corroborates these insights in the sequences that interlace cannibalism and carnivory and in Pi's demonstration of what it means to "eat well." In the first story, Pi eats human flesh after Richard Parker kills a man also adrift, blind, and starving in the Pacific Ocean. At this point in the novel, they have not yet discovered the island, and Pi and Richard Parker are "two emaciated mammals, parched and starving. Richard Parker's fur lost its lustre, and some of it even fell away from his shoulders and haunches. He lost a lot of weight, became a skeleton in an oversized bag of faded fur. I, too, withered away, the moistness sucked out of me, my bones showing plainly through my thin flesh" (239). Both are blind when a voice responds to Pi's death's-door goodbye and prayer, a voice Pi initially thinks is Richard Parker's until he confusedly realizes the voice has a French accent. After exchanging stories about food, the two humans pull their boats alongside each other and the other man grabs Pi, probably to eat him. Instead, Richard Parker "ripped the flesh off the man's frame and cracked his bones" (255) and both tiger and boy eat his body in a feast of carnivory and cannibalism. Pi confesses, "I ate some of his flesh. I mean small pieces, little strips that I meant for the gaff's hook that, when dried by the sun, looked like ordinary animal flesh. They slipped into my mouth nearly unnoticed. You must understand, my suffering was unremitting and he was already dead. I stopped as soon as I caught a fish. I pray for his soul every day" (256). Meat is meat, and cannibalism in this version of the story is a result of opportunity and necessity, as is *all* meat eating for Pi.

The second version of Pi's story, the one without animals, further highlights the essential materiality of human beings through its alignment of the cannibalistic and the carnivorous. Within days of the Tsimsum's sinking, the sailor dies (probably from blood loss after the cook amputated his rotting leg to use as bait), and the cook eats him. The cook's cannibalism is unnecessary when the human survivors still have resources in the boat and a bounty of fish, turtles, and other creatures in the ocean below. In parallel, Pi and his mother, previously vegetarians, begin eating fish and turtle meat. After the

---

[30] Ibid., 81.

cook kills Pi's mother, Pi stabs him in an unbelievable burst of energy and eats his flesh, saying "his heart was a struggle—all those tubes that connected it. I managed to get it out. It tasted delicious, far better than turtle. I ate his liver. I cut off great pieces of his flesh" (311). The previously sharp categorical cut marking ethical types of eating—Pi's vegetarianism—is rendered obsolete and irrelevant: no flesh to animal flesh to human flesh. What of Pi's core values? What of his vegetarianism, his gentle pacifism? One of the terrible realities of the second story is not just the loss and suffering, but the transformation of Pi himself. "Lord, to think that I'm a strict vegetarian. To think that when I was a child I always shuddered when I snapped open a banana because it sounded to me like the breaking of an animal's neck. I descended to a level of savagery I never imagined possible" (197). Animals and those we animalize are indispensable in ethical systems that maintain human exceptionalisms, but Pi does not distinguish animal and human when it comes to eating flesh. He does distinguish between the motivations for killing. In the case of the cook's hyena-like qualities, the motivations are sinister and selfish, as is, perhaps, Pi's own revenge. However, a hyena eating a zebra is just doing what a hyena does. What does it mean to be human? The novel obliterates the distinctions. We can only conclude that all sustenance is murder, but there is a way to eat well. By admitting that we are absolutely no different, that human exceptionalism is a lie, we can move toward a position of solidarity with the rest of the living world.

In contrast to this reading, Graham Huggan and Helen Tiffin evoke the inter-implication of carnivory and cannibalism in *Postcolonial Ecocriticism: Literature, Animals, Environment* to contend that murder and cannibalism only occur after the human shipwreck survivors have become bestial so as to maintain the species boundary. They claim that Pi attributes unethical behavior to humans who have been animalized, concluding that instances of "Human cannibalism turns people into 'animals' or 'beasts,' but without jeopardising human distinctiveness."[31] Indeed, it is true that Pi's mother exclaims, "You monster! You animal! How could you? He's *human!*" in the second story when she catches the cook slipping a piece of the sailor

---

[31]   Graham Huggan and Helen Tiffin, *Postcolonial Ecocriticism: Literature, Animals, Environment* (New York: Routledge, 2010), 173.

into his mouth, but the next line speaks volumes: "He's your own kind!" (308). Within the structures of Hindu and Buddhist vegetarianism and pacifism, all beings are sacred life, one's "own kind." Accordingly, what is most profound about *Life of Pi*'s accomplishment here is the utter revision of Cartesian dualisms that trouble such binary constructions as animal/human and self/other. Furthermore, cannibalism—at least symbolically—is a core ritual in Christian religious practice in the replication of the Lord's Supper in communion ceremonies, and the Frenchman is a Christ figure in the scene where blind, weakened Pi eats his body, is baptized in his tears, and regains his sight. In fresh intersubjective connectedness, Pi celebrates and is like Christ, "who goes hungry, who suffers from thirst, who gets tired, who is sad, who is anxious, who is heckled and harassed, who has to put up with followers who don't get it and opponents who don't respect Him" (55). It is too simplistic to suggest that cannibalism is equivalent to animality.

I return to the irreducible entanglement of religions here to demonstrate one of the ways that Pi fulfills Haraway's call to "be good, that is, to deserve a future."[32] Earlier I argued that the cohesive harmony of Pi's three claimed religions—Hinduism, Christianity, and Islam—is woven in Pi's conception of his faith to combat hierarchical thinking and the limitations of language. As with any thread of analysis about *Life of Pi*, however, it is actually much more complicated than that: the theme of faith in this novel forms five points around an empty space that symbolizes the kind of arrogance and lack of humility Haraway might consider not-good or undeserving, agnostics. To be clear, it is not the religiosity itself that matters, but the willingness to humble the self in the face of something bigger and inarticulate that I argue is represented in this novel via systems of faith that indicate Pi's mortal and moral entanglements. The five points are signified by Atheism, Judaism, and the Hinduism, Christianity, and Islam we have already explored. Judaism is only alluded to briefly in the name of Isaac Luria, about whom Pi wrote his religious studies undergraduate thesis, and in the name of the sunken ship, Tsimtsum, yet those clues point us toward important ways the novel further maps the blurring of boundaries and the questions of ethical relations with other beings we have been examining so far. Known as "the Lion," Luria (who

---

[32] Haraway, *When Species Meet*, 106.

lived from 1534 to 1572) constructed a cosmogony that describes how God leaves room for humankind by withdrawing divine energy while still being present at a reduced wattage, so to speak, that allows imperfection a space to exist (the issue being how an infinite and perfect deity can make room for finite and imperfect beings). Creation is thus a divine contraction. The contraction of divinity is called tzimtzum, the diminution or concealment that brings into being the finite world and humankind and allows for the messy imperfection of free will.[33] Atheism is believing that there is no deity and seems an odd kind of "faith" to Pi, but he notes that atheists are "brothers and sisters of a different faith, and every word they speak speaks of faith. Like me, they go as far as the legs of reason will carry them—and then they leap" (28). In contrast, agnostics are indecisive and put doubt at the center of their existence instead of an inarticulable divinity. As Pi puts it, "To choose doubt as a philosophy of life is akin to choosing immobility as a means of transportation" (28). In so doing, agnostics both reinscribe and reify hierarchies of being that centralize the importance of the human over all others and "end up believing in nothing and having worthless dreams" (xii). Within agnostic hierarchies of human exceptionalism, there is no way to "eat well."

The final chapters of *Life of Pi* ask readers to take a leap of faith. Rather than a singular, monolithic answer, readers must interrogate the ambiguity of three viable, plausible scenarios that destabilize our notions of reality. Foreshadowed by Pi's initial disbelief about the Christ story ("What a downright weird story. What peculiar psychology. I asked for another story, one that I might find more satisfying" [53]), in the final chapters the Japanese investigators are unable to believe the first story, his fantastic journey of survival with Richard Parker. Initially the two officials challenge his claim that Orange-Juice, the orangutan, survived the sinking of the Tsimtsum on a mass of floating bananas because bananas sink (they do not—I tested this myself, apparently also guilty of incredulity). Then they question the fidelity of the island, claiming it is "botanically impossible" (295). So are bonsai trees, Pi retorts. Finally they assert that there is "no trace" of Richard Parker in Mexico (296) and thus "don't believe there was a tiger" in the lifeboat with Pi (297).

---

[33] See chabad.org for more about Jewish mysticism and tzimtzum.

Frustrated, Pi erupts: "Don't you bully me with your politeness! Love is hard to believe, ask any lover. Life is hard to believe, ask any scientist. God is hard to believe, ask any believer. What is your problem with hard to believe?" (297). Pi is pressured to revoke his first report and tell the "truth" about his experiences, the Japanese officials desiring a story "that will confirm what you already know. That won't make you see higher or further or differently. You want a flat story. An immobile story. You want dry, yeastless factuality. You want a story without animals" (302–3). Pi gives them the second story of human ruthlessness and violence. And woven in is the third, the story often ignored or missed by readers and scholars, summed up in one sentence: "In both stories, the ship sinks, my entire family dies, and I suffer" (317).

The impulse to cultivate a singular notion of reality is a very Western humanist one, but one that the entirety of this novel decenters, queering the notions of duality and human exceptionalism and replacing them with simultaneity, as I have been arguing. What does it say about our humanity that we are willing to believe the more horrific story over the more extraordinary one?[34] Is this doubt an inability to believe in the spectacular, a comment on our pervasive lack of imagination and willingness to miss the better story and have worthless dreams? Although scholars have probed and prodded *Life of Pi* in hopes of unraveling the novel to reveal one grand metanarrative, Capital "T" Truth, what critical scholarship has thus far failed to address is that believing in all the stories simultaneously, in having "faith" in *all* the ways of being, is the path toward an answer to the question of whether this is a novel that will make anyone believe in infinite possibilities (the "God" promised by Mr. Adirubasamy). In storytelling itself lies the answer. It is what ties everything together: sloths, the infinitude of Pi, religiosity, tzimtzum, human and animal, truth and fiction. Rather than floating aimlessly like agnostics, readers can revel in all the stories and all the ways of being, no matter how whimsical or frightening. We become like Yashoda peering into the toddler Krishna's mouth:

> She sees in Krishna's mouth the whole complete entire timeless universe,
> all the stars and planets of space and the distance between them, all the

---

[34] In a parallel construction, is climate change "believable"?

lands and seas of the earth and the life in them; she sees all the days of yesterday and all the days of tomorrow; she sees all ideas and all emotions, all pity and all hope, and the three strands of matter; not a pebble, candle, creature, village or galaxy is missing, including herself and every bit of dirt in its truthful place. (55)

To claim the exactitude of Truth with any certainty would be to reassume a dominance, to reinscribe the very hierarchical structures of human exceptionalism and independence that Martel has so artfully undone in this novel, wherein from the beginning the shape of it refuses to come to any concrete resolution about sustainability, survival, truth, reality, or even fiction and nonfiction. For example, the "Author's Note" provides essential background information for making sense of the later italicized authorial interventions. In it, we are introduced to a writer with plans to set his next book in Portugal in 1939 who travels to Bombay to alleviate his writer's block. Once there, he realizes that his book "all adds up to nothing" and mails it to a fictional address (viii).[35] He then travels to Pondicherry, where he is told about Pi Patel's story—the one "that will make [him] believe in God" (x). The whole concept of a fictional book set up to be a nonfiction story framed by a fictional author writing a biography about Pi Patel challenges the ideas of truth and reality that come to fruition again in the three versions of Pi's adventure. All is intersubjective connectedness, woven bricolage, trans-corporeal embeddedness within the fully fleshed world.

As such, *Life of Pi* models the rejuvenation of *empathy* as a human animal subject within an ecocollapsed world, one living as "another body engaged in the world," becoming, to use the words of David Abram, "a two-legged animal, entirely a part of the animate world whose life swells within and unfolds all around us [that] seeks a new way of speaking, one that enacts our interbeing with the earth rather than blinding us to it [and] opens our sense to the sensuous in all its multiform strangeness."[36] Like Pi, we must face the density and complexity of global warming and its manifold transformations at multiple, entangled, and multiply enfolding simultaneous levels of engagement. There is no singular story. In *Life of Pi*, human extinction is one

35   Is the manuscript lost in a sea of mail?
36   David Abram, *Becoming Animal: An Earthly Cosmology* (New York: Pantheon Books, 2010), 3.

of "human" extinction: the human individual no longer exists as a unified subject independent of the rest of the living and nonliving world. However, for Pi there is a Mexico to provide succor, so the following chapter explores what happens when there is no escape from ecocollapse, when the two-legged animal bodies literally join those of other species going extinct.

3

The Last Stragglers of Ecocollapse: "Diary of an Interesting Year" and *The Road*

Although Pi Patel's experience in *Life of Pi* alludes to the contemporary fantasy that there will be a climate change solution, a metaphorical Mexico for our species' escape craft to colonize, other ecocollapse fiction destabilizes that trope by presenting realistic unlivable global ecosystems and devastated personal landscapes. Such speculations leave no hope for rescue or long-term species survival while making visible the precarity that falls most heavily on vulnerable populations. Helen Simpson's "Diary of an Interesting Year" (2012), originally published in the *New Yorker*,[1] presents readers with a female narrator who rejects the social contract, subverting the violent suppression of agency seen in ecocollapse fictions like Cormac McCarthy's *The Road* (2006) even as an unlivable earth becomes a site that refutes human species regeneration. This kind of ecocollapse fiction destabilizes futuristic notions of the world into something fundamentally uninhabitable for the human species, challenging the concepts of human superiority while providing no lifeboat, no escape to another planet, and no effective climate solution. Human exceptionalism, marked by traditional dualistic frameworks, dissolves utterly in "Diary of an Interesting Year" and *The Road*, their entanglements revealed in the dissonances between survivors' lived experiences and oppositional constructions from the past. The feminist reframing of vulnerability in "Diary" and the enculturation of cannibalism in *The Road* incorporate epistemological ruptures that break down notions of good/bad, civilized/barbaric, culture/nature, and human/

---

[1] Reprinted with slight modifications in *In-Flight Entertainment: Stories* (2012) and in Mark Martin's collection *I'm with the Bears: Short Stories from a Damaged Planet* (2011).

animal, placing humans firmly within the biological sphere rather than elevated above it in an artificial hierarchy of human exceptionalism.

Simpson's "Diary of an Interesting Year," set in 2040, enables a deep emersion into the dying ecosystem as civilization breaks down via the brief journal entries written by the unnamed narrator in her thirtieth-birthday present. There is no intricate plot, and the depth and length of diary entries decrease as the story progresses, indicating both the increasing simplification of daily living (eventually to pure biological survival) and the pages running out (the only exception being the final entry, with which she purposefully fills the last page of her journal). The first indication that there is something amiss in the year 2040 is the description of her gift: "This little spiral-backed notebook and a Biro. It's a good present, hardly any rust on the spiral and no water damage to the paper."[2] In what world is a rusted spiral notebook and a ballpoint pen a good gift? In the world of shortages "after the Big Melt" (146), when there is no hot water, no internet, and no electricity; cities are inundated with cholera; and the closure of hospitals and implementation of travel restrictions make nearly every illness a deadly affliction. Arguing for a reading of the uncanny in "Diary," Gregers Andersen makes the point that "in cli-fi, the animated, revengeful, nonhuman entity . . . marks the end of the idea that the nonhuman world is a God-given space for human mastery populated with Cartesian objects."[3] Human exceptionalism finds no purchase in the ecocollapsed world. The narrator's husband, called only "G," had been her university tutor, and they quarrel about what she describes as "wall-to-wall pontificating from an older man" about how he saw it all coming (146). "They should carve it on his tombstone," she gripes. "I Was Right" (144). We know only that she has "ribs like a fence, hair in greasy rats' tails" (145). Despite being highly educated, middle-class, and able-bodied people, neither of them have any particular skills or knowledge that will facilitate their survival in this frightening, ecocollapsed world.

"Diary" thus points toward what environmental justice activists have identified as institutionalized sacrifice zones wherein environmental burdens are unequally placed on disempowered and marginalized communities while

---

[2] Helen Simpson, "Diary of an Interesting Year," in *In-Flight Entertainment: Stories* (New York: Alfred A. Knopf, 2012), 144. Subsequent citations appear parenthetically in the text.
[3] Gregers Andersen, "Cli-Fi and the Uncanny," *ISLE: Interdisciplinary Studies in Literature and Environment* 23, no. 4 (Autumn 2016): 860.

shifting the categorical cut to include even more people than readers might expect. The remnants of government are barely present, visible only through the instructions to wear face masks (in the March 2 entry), then rationing (March 6), a reduced government food delivery and compulsory billeting announcement (June 6), an Army truck delivering refugees (July 1), a radio announcement disabling all civilian cars (August 9), and finally, in the August 16 entry, the note that "all the farmland round here is surrounded by razor wire and armed guards" (153). There may be some hope for "the top layer" for whom that food is probably intended because they are "hanging on inside their plastic bubbles of filtered air while the rest of us shuffle about with goiters and tumors and bits of old sheet tied over our mouths" (146), but after the March 6 entry the super-privileged also disappear: it is unclear if even the least marginalized individuals can survive in the short term. Filtered air requires a functioning infrastructure that rapidly disintegrates.

The intersections of human subjectivity and scientific instrumentalism are visible and devastating. The significant environmental collapse is a result of anthropogenic climate changes and no human efforts can halt it. The earth can no longer sustain human life: "Thresholds crossed, cascade effect, [we were] hopelessly optimistic to assume we had till 2060" (146), the narrator tells us; the "rivers and streams [are] all toxic—fertilizers, typhoid, etc." (152). To drink they must bleach and boil water, only consuming what moisture steams onto a T-shirt stretched over a pot. Someone has deliberately manipulated the planetary environment to counteract changes in atmospheric chemistry, and "Weeping sores on hands and faces" are "unfortunate side effects of cloud seeding" (154). Simpson valuably problematizes geoengineering, which is frequently touted as a potential solution to global climate change. Intentional weather modification is common around airports and can be accomplished with silver iodide and solid carbon dioxide (dry ice) to induce precipitation or suppress hail or fog. In California, these efforts intensified because of a multiyear drought, although "The Turlock district has partnered with the neighboring Modesto Irrigation District to seed the Sierra's Tuolumne River watershed off and on for the past 25 years."[4] Other forms of geoengineering

---

[4] Kurtis Alexander, "Pilots 'Seed' Clouds, Fighting the Drought from the Sky," *The San Francisco Chronicle*, April 3, 2016.

include carbon dioxide removal via ocean fertilization and solar radiation management, composed largely of various methods of reflection, including stratospheric sulfur aerosol release. Field research is underway in China, Great Britain, the United States, and elsewhere. The sulfate aerosols that might stabilize global temperatures are a pollutant, and they can theoretically be sprayed into the atmosphere without regulation by any company or government entity.[5] However, climate change is not purely a physical problem resolvable with a technical solution, as Simpson makes clear. The protected farmland, cut through by toxic rivers, cannot provide edible crops for long. Even the trees are dead and falling: "Rare dry afternoon. Black lace clouds over yellow sky. Brown grass, frowsty gray mold, fungal frills. Dead trees come crashing down without warning—one nearly got us today, it made us jump" (153). Although weather modification might seem a reasonable solution to rampant temperature shifts, extreme technologies can have extreme—and unexpected—consequences.

Because they are dependent on a reliable news source, the people isolated in cities cannot know the status of the world outside. After their bedroom is taken over by billeted Spaniards and their stash of tinned food is discovered and consumed, G and the narrator decide their best course of action is to head toward Russia, hoping it might be "the new land of milk and honey since the Big Melt" (155). The next billet will be arriving from distant Tehran, though, so readers know their escape is futile—the whole world is already uninhabitable. On foot, sleeping in a pop-up tent and avoiding the roads where there is a greater chance of being arrested or mugged, they discover they cannot do anything useful in this confusing new world. When they encounter a thin, sick pig, G exclaims:

> "Quick! We've got to kill it!"
>
> "Why?" I said. "How?"
>
> "With a knife," he said. "Bacon. Sausages."

---

[5] Excellent reports about current geoengineering projects and their potential dangers include the Royal Society's "Geoengineering the Climate: Science, Governance, and Uncertainty," published studies by the United States' National Research Council, Eli Kintisch's "'Asilomar 2' Takes Small Steps Toward Rules for Geoengineering," and Johnathan Watts's "US and Saudi Arabia Blocking Regulation of Geoengineering, Sources Say."

I pointed out that even if we managed to stab it to death with our old kitchen knife, which seemed unlikely, we wouldn't be able just to open it up and find bacon and sausages inside.

"Milk, then!" G said wildly. "It's a mammal, isn't it?"

Meanwhile, the pig walked off. (154)

Here Simpson satirizes high-carbon society's dependence on technology, industrial agriculture, and the invisible production of meat, which is completely severed from the animals killed so their flesh can be eaten. The narrator and G are well-educated fools, retaining human exceptionalism as conceived in the humanist tradition. They leave their apartment with a tent, sleeping bags, and a wind-up radio, planning to gather sustenance from the dead world around them, but there is no food. Although they imagined finding "damsons, blackberries, young green nettles for soup" (153), all they have actually eaten is chickweed and ivy. The only other living creatures are squirrels, rats, pigeons, and insects. G knows pigs are the source of bacon and sausages and also knows that their bodies must be processed in some way to become food, but he does not know how to do any of it. His pitiful desperation becomes a forewarning of his (and our?) inadequate engagement with the materiality of intra-active ecosystems. The invisibility of how the absent referent's process of "violently transforming living animals to dead consumable ones" powerfully inverts.[6]

Their inability to read the physical landscape extends to a blindness toward cultural landscapes as well. They are unable to protect themselves physically in a world where their cultural norms and expectations no longer apply: G and the narrator are disoriented at the lability of social niceties back in their apartment and the anomie they experience leaves them ill-equipped to deal with a normless ecocollapsed social situation. When the climate refugees first arrive, for example, they show them around and are shocked and confused when the Spanish grandmother immediately takes over their bedroom, leaving them to sleep on the kitchen table, assuming that the hospitality that previously oriented homeowner and houseguest applies in their current situation. They likewise cannot read the cultural environment outside their apartment, pushing their lone bicycle across the countryside to wake up on

---

[6] Carol Adams, *The Sexual Politics of Meat: A Feminist-Vegetarian Critical Theory* (New York: Continuum, 1996), 47.

the fourth morning and discover it stolen. "Could be worse," G says. "We could have had our throats cut while we slept" (152). Even after such fortuitous luck, there is no indication they recognize their bodily vulnerability. Instead, G cries and wishes for a gun. As Jane Elliott argues in "Suffering Agency," "When life is reduced to minimal elements and self-preservation is at stake, . . . the subject's interest in preserving his or her life leads to limit-case decisions and deeds that would be otherwise unthinkable."[7] Would G, a university tutor, be able to kill someone? Under what circumstances?

In "Diary of an Interesting Year," the bedroom ownership is about both power and sexual possession, extending deeper than just a matter of space or privacy: "G depressed. The four Spaniards are bigger than him, and he's worried that the biggest one, Miguel, has his eye on me" (150). Within six weeks of leaving the apartment, G is murdered by a man with a gun, and the narrator is taken captive as M's (for murderer?) sex slave and potential food source. M "turned everything else inside out (including me)" after killing G. "What he does to me is horrible," the narrator tells us. "M can't seem to get through the day without at least two blow jobs. I'm always sick afterward (sometimes during)" (156). When she tries to escape, he beats her up. One night he bites her repeatedly and leaves bleeding wounds she licks clean, "just meat on legs to him" (157). Their inability to communicate undoubtedly makes things worse because they are together but isolated: "M speaks another language. Norwegian? Dutch? Croatian? We can't talk, so he hits me instead" (156). Thus, the patriarchal possession of the narrator's sexual and physical body passes from G to M, although as we see, she finally takes ownership of it herself.

The inescapability of sexual violence for female characters within the larger state of social anarchy is a common feature of post-apocalyptic fiction. Judith Butler notes that

> Women and minorities, including sexual minorities, are, as a community, subjected to violence, exposed to its possibility, if not its realization. This means that each of us is constituted politically in part by virtue of the social vulnerability of our bodies—as a site of desire and physical vulnerability, as a

---

[7] Jane Elliott, "Suffering Agency: Imagined Neoliberal Personhood in North America and Britain," *Social Text* (115) 31, no. 2 (Summer 2013): 89.

site of a publicity at once assertive and exposed. Loss and vulnerability seem to follow from our being socially constituted bodies, attached to others, at risk of losing those attachments, exposed to others, at risk of violence by virtue of that exposure.[8]

Rape is an assault on bodily integrity and the sexual expression of power and anger. It is also a method of control and re-empowerment for some men in situations of vulnerability and stress that oppresses and objectifies women, as revealed in Susan Brownmiller's groundbreaking book *Against Our Will: Men, Women, and Rape* (which reframed all future discussions of sexual assault). Although controversial among feminist scholars, Brownmiller's argument is useful when we consider that the post-apocalyptic scenarios imagined in fictional texts in many ways replicate the chaos, fear, and danger of war. She contends,

> War provides men with the perfect psychological backdrop to give vent to their contempt for women. The very maleness of the military—the brute power of weaponry exclusive to their hands, the spiritual bonding of men at arms, the manly discipline of orders given and orders obeyed, the simple logic of the hierarchical command—confirms for men what they long suspect, that women are peripheral, irrelevant to the world that counts, passive spectators to the action in the center ring.[9]

Sexual assault further reinforces the sense of superiority of the rapist and is an "act men do in the name of their masculinity," not an act of sex but an act of domination (312). In *Behave: The Biology of Humans at Our Best and Worst* (2017), Robert Sapolsky confirms Brownmiller's position, referring to violent assault in times of trauma and stress as a form of "displacement aggression" that reduces physiological stress chemicals in the aggressor.[10] Ann Cahill complicates Brownmiller's argument in *Rethinking Rape*, where she contends that "If we understand the feminine body both as a site for the inscription of patriarchal and misogynist truths and as a fluid, indeterminate set of possibilities, we can address the complexity of

---

[8] Judith Butler, *Precarious Life: The Powers of Mourning and Violence* (London: Verso, 2004), 20.
[9] Susan Brownmiller, *Against Our Will: Men, Women, and Rape* (New York: Ballentine Books, 1975), 32.
[10] Robert M. Sapolsky, *Behave: The Biology of Humans at Our Best and Worst* (New York: Penguin Books, 2017), 132.

rape without overdetermining women as victims"[11] and argues that doing so makes possible the recognition of women's agency and acts of resistance. In apocalyptic and post-apocalyptic literature, some authors write back to expose the reduction of women to mere objects of male violence and lust during times of turmoil and, valuably, reveal how differences among people situate them very differently in the context of sexual violence. For example, Eva and Nell abandon civilization entirely after a violent rape in Jean Hegland's *Into the Forest* (1998). In Stephen King's *The Stand*, Dayna, Susan, Shirley, and other women are enslaved and drugged so they can be "repeatedly raped, sodomized, and forced to perform fellatio" on their captors[12] but eventually escape, killing their rapists. Octavia Butler's *Parable of the Sower* (1993) is practically a catalog of sexual horrors that leads the protagonist, Lauren, to enact situational transgender performativity to protect herself: A young naked woman's dazed expression leads Lauren to ponder, "Maybe she had been raped so much that she was crazy. I'd heard stories of that happening."[13] She sees a little girl in the street, "naked, maybe seven years old with blood running down her bare thighs" (13). Mrs. Sims is raped: "An old lady like that!" (32). There is "Little Robin Balter, naked, filthy, bloody between her legs, cold, bony, barely pubescent"; Layla Yannis, also raped; Lidia Cruz, only eight years old, "raped, too" (163). Lauren wisely decides the safest thing is to dress and behave like a man (although not a rapist) as she leads her people toward a new, more empathetic civilization.

In contrast to the frequency of male-on-female rape, sexual domination only occasionally occurs against a male character in these fictions. In *The Stand*, The Kid sodomizes Trashcan Man with a pistol in a rare example of sexual violence against a man:

> Whatever it was suddenly pressing against his anus, it wasn't flesh. It was cold steel.
>
> And suddenly he *knew* what it was.

---

[11]   Ann Cahill, *Rethinking Rape* (Ithaca: Cornell University Press, 1993), 13.
[12]   Stephen King, *The Stand: The Complete and Uncut Version* (1990; repr., New York: Anchor Books, 2011), 689.
[13]   Octavia Butler, *Parable of the Sower* (New York: Grand Central Publishing, 1993), 9. Subsequent citations appear parenthetically in the text.

"No," he whispered. His eyes were wide and terrified in the dark. Now he could dimly see that homicidal doll's face in the mirror, hanging over his shoulder with its hair in its red eyes.

"Yes," The Kid whispered back. "And you don't want to lose a stroke, Trashy. Not one motherfuckin stroke. Or I might just pull the trigger on this thang. Blow your shitfactory all to hell and gone. Dumdums, Trashy. You believe that happy crappy?" (740)

The Kid's depravity conveys his domination and control over Trashcan Man and deepens his characterization as an evil, violent person.[14] Nonetheless, it is far more common in this tradition to read of women being raped than of men as part of larger narratives of us/them othering.

In "Diary," readers witness the narrator as both the victim of other people's othering and the perpetrator of it when protecting her own continued existence, a complexity not often found in climate fiction's easy dependence on binary oppositions that underlie hierarchies of individualism and human exceptionalism. Specifically, violence and rape are just the immediate horrors of being held captive, but pregnancy is the ongoing hazard and is a greater fear to the narrator than rape or other bodily harm (as evidenced in part by the number of diary entries: fourteen of the forty-two mention pregnancy while only five address sexual violence). At first, the entries speak to the inconvenience of washing diapers when there is no hot water or proper detergent: "At least I haven't got to do nappies, like Lexi or Esme—that would send me right over the edge" (147). When the narrator has trouble sleeping, she commands herself to "Think of something nice. Soap and hot water. Fresh air. Condoms! Sick of being permanently on knife edge re pregnancy" (147–8). Finally, though, readers get a fuller understanding of what pregnancy can mean for women of childbearing age when there is no medical care, no midwives, and no knowledge source without the internet:

17th July 2040 Maia died yesterday. It was horrible. The baby got stuck two weeks ago, it died inside her. Astrid Huggins was useless, she didn't have a

---

[14] Further evidence of the unusual nature of male-on-male sexual assault in this genre is the critical reaction to it. For example, Tony Magistrale labels Trashcan Man's rape "sadomasochistic perversions of Trashcan Man and The Kid" (33), as though Trashcan Man is a consenting but submissive party to his own sexual assault. See "Free Will and Sexual Choice in *The Stand*," *Extrapolation* 34, no. 1 (1993): 30–8.

clue. Martin started waving his Swiss penknife round on the second day and yelling about a cesarean, he had to be dragged off her. He's at our place now drinking the last of our precious brandy with the Spaniards. (151)

Privileged, educated Westerners have specialized and technologized themselves out of being capable of surviving something as routine and "natural" as pregnancy, which, while never without risks, has a much lower maternal and infant mortality rate with prenatal and birthing care. Distributive injustices present in global capitalism's many inequities are leveled in "Diary."

Moreover, traditional abortion methods are a mystery. Licking her bite wounds in October, the narrator remembers "how nice the taste of blood is, how I miss it. Strength. Calves' liver for iron. How I haven't had a period for ages. When that thought popped out I missed a beat. Then my blood ran cold" (157). Pregnancy brings more than potential death for her: it also is certain death for the child. We are told that the Hatchwells' two sons died the year before, and the narrator gives a new baby "three months max in these conditions. Diarrhea, basically" (147), a point made before she left the relative cleanliness of the apartment. Even if she survives birthing a child, there is no chance they will both live; the baby will most certainly die, likely killing her in the process, like it did Maia. However, she cannot search the internet to learn how to abort the fetus. "Wasn't it juniper berries they used to use? As in gin? Even if it was, I wouldn't know what they looked like—I remember only mint and basil. I can't be pregnant. I won't be pregnant" (157). Later she is "Very sick after drinking rank juice off random stewed herbs. Nothing else, though, worse luck" (157). Finally, she tricks M into kicking her violently and repeatedly by pretending she drank some of his vodka and thus induces a painful miscarriage. She then shoves the drunk M off the tree platform where he was keeping her captive and notes that, although she heard him groan for at least three days, he is finally dead.

Whereas typical climate change fictions follow apocalyptic and post-apocalyptic generic conventions by establishing simple oppositions between "good" and "evil" in their constructed worlds, "Diary of an Interesting Year" points to the complex, slippery, and even contradictory nature of goodness and badness—perhaps especially so in a devastated, ecocollapsed landscape where there is no hope for species survival. Sexual violence in this story may be characteristic of the post-apocalyptic genre, yet Simpson's project seems all the more valuable for her attempts to demonstrate M's subjectivity instead of instituting a more reflexive gesture by unsophisticatedly dismissing him as an inhumane monster and thus allowing readers to draw a definitive line between "us" (and the narrator) and "them" (all others). Instead, readers witness that the emotional trauma of ecocollapse is felt by everyone, even the abusive M: "He was singing and sobbing and carrying on" mourning his losses, whatever they may specifically be (159). While M dehumanizes the narrator and she dehumanizes him, we are forced into a profound grappling with the impulse to other, exclude, stigmatize, and abuse other people based not only on some trait or characteristic for which they bear no responsibility (sex, ethnicity, nationality, etc.) but beyond that in the narrative, simply because an other *exists*. The existence of any other human being in this environment reduces one's own chance of survival. M's selfish, sexually brutal, and violent behavior toward the narrator marks him as evil and cruel, as does his murder of her husband G. But we cannot simply ask, "Who is the murderer? Who has no mercy?" and exclude the protagonist herself. She not only shoves him from the tree (which is self-defense, certainly) but she is unnecessarily cruel, allowing M to suffer for three days after falling from the platform when she could charitably execute him with the gun she now possesses. Instead of judging her, though, readers sense the moral murkiness at play here: is altruism an unaffordable luxury? The sorts of cultural trappings that encourage selflessness fall away as she proceeds further and further away from the city, just as they surely do for M. The abuse of the vulnerable—a foundation of patriarchal, capitalistic power structures—encourages those people not temporarily saved by status and money to fight each other for their own, individual survival, as singular exceptions amid the rule of human extinction.

The ending is puzzling and complex, full of images that are reassuring and unsettling at the same time:

13th November 2040 I've wrapped your remains in my good blue shirt; sorry I couldn't let you stay on board, but there's no future now for any baby aboveground. I'm the end of the line!

This is the last page of my thirtieth birthday present. When I've finished it I'll wrap the notebook up in six plastic bags, sealing each one with duct tape against the rain, then I'll bury it in a hole on top of the blue shirt. I don't know why, as I'm not mad enough to think anybody will ever read it. After that I'm going to buckle on this rucksack of provisions and head north with my gun. Wish me luck. Last line: Good luck, good luck, good luck, good luck, good luck. (159)

Like a prayer said over and over, "Good luck" becomes the mantra of a journey that readers can only imagine. The narrator could choose to make a home of the platform (M had stored plenty of canned foods and water) but rejects domesticity, becoming—ironically, perhaps—the "woman on the run" best known in US fiction as a male figure escaping emasculating civilization for the restorative freedom of wilderness. In contrast, she seeks the potentially more hospitable north and will continually have to find food, water, and shelter in the ecocollapsed ruins while remaining undiscovered by other people trying likewise to survive.

Although the ending feels a little hopeful because we are reading it so that we experience it as though someone survives, readers cannot help but wonder: what good is good luck in a violent, ecocollapsed world? The answer to that question might be found in another realistic post-apocalyptic fiction that imagines ecocollapse and extinction and thus might help us imagine the unnamed narrator's future as she escapes the city: *The Road* by Cormac McCarthy. This now-famous tale of an unnamed boy and his father trekking south through a deadened landscape has been described by Andrew Tate, who interprets it via tropes of walking, as one that "resonates with a distinctively early twenty-first-century history in which thousands of people are forced out of their homes as a result of war, starvation and environmental crisis."[15] Nothing grows; ash falls everywhere; it is difficult to imagine a less hospitable landscape. All they can hope for is "No more balefires on the distant ridges. He thought the bloodcults must have all consumed one another. No one traveled this road. No roadagents, no marauders."[16] The absolute truth of the world is "darkness implacable. The blind dogs of the sun in their running. The crushing black vacuum of the universe. And

---

[15] Andrew Tate, *Apocalyptic Fiction* (London: Bloomsbury, 2017), 90. Subsequent citations appear parenthetically in the text.
[16] Cormac McCarthy, *The Road* (New York: Vintage Books, 2006), 16. Subsequent citations appear parenthetically in the text.

somewhere two hunted animals trembling like groundfoxes in their cover. Borrowed time and borrowed world and borrowed eyes with which to sorrow it" (130). The father can only motivate his son to keep walking, keep hoping that something might be different further south, and be prepared for the moment where he might have to use his one bullet to kill his own child. As Shelly L. Rambo argues, "McCarthy catches the reader in a schizophrenic, and distinctively American, post-apocalyptic crisis of meaning: between the craving for a happy ending (for resolution, for redemption) and the recognition of its impossibility (there is, in Christian terms, no resurrection ahead)."[17] Even the ease with which we understand mutually exclusive states like "alive" and "dead" is shown to be false here. What does it mean to be alive in a dead ecosystem?

These permeable, fluid relations between self and others are reified in the issues of cannibalism raised in these fictions. Cannibalism here forms boundaries and dissolves them and defines and redefines what it means to be a human being, creating and subverting normative boundaries simultaneously. While cannibalism plays a significant role in how we think about difference and its relation to definitions of identity and selfhood, in *The Road* it also demonstrates that the fuzzy mutable logic of anti-cannibalistic morality does not provide recourse in the ecocollapsed world. Whereas Simpson's narrator is "just meat on legs" (157) to her captor, in *The Road* the dual fears of cannibalism are present: both the fear of being cannibalized and the fear of becoming cannibal. But there is no civilization left for the father to contrast against the barbarity of cannibalism despite his efforts to do so; rather, there are just the practical matters motivated by the concrete logic of hunger and satiation. Thus, other people become both a source of terror and an object of desire. Many scholars have addressed the way the unnamed man insists to his son that they are the "good guys" and will never eat another human, instead "carrying the fire" that Paul Patton explains is "a metaphor for some kind of moral order

---

[17] Shelly L. Rambo, "Beyond Redemption? Reading Cormac McCarthy's *The Road* After the End of the World," *Studies in the Literary Imagination* 41, no. 2 (Fall 2008): 101. Fascinatingly, however, many scholars *do* see redemption and a revival of hope in the novel. For example, one reviewer called it "a tale of survival and the miracle of goodness" (quoted in James Wood, "Getting to the End," 47). See also works by Nels Anchor Christensen, Ashley Kunsa, D. Marcel DeCoste, Geoff Hamilton, Hannah Stark, James Wood, Stefan Skrimshire, and Thomas H. Schaub, among many others.

and the guarantee of some future humanity that is clearly intended, at least in the eyes of the father, to be borne by the son."[18] But "the fire" is inadequate: the boy recognizes the complexity of eating and being eaten, concerned even that the unfair division of food—the father gives the boy a greater share—is a form of cannibalism. Arielle Zibrak shows that the boy interprets that inequity as "structural cannibalism that he and his father are doomed to practice on one another."[19] What I want to do, instead, is explore cannibalism from an unbiased perspective by examining the marauding road rats, the supposed "bad guys" who eat human meat. This move requires a strategic reframing that recognizes the road rats not as evil but as hungry, as human animals having adapted to the new world, as a logical extension of the carnivorous structure of othering outlined in Chapter 1 and that we already incorporate in factory farms where the meat industry treats nonhuman animals, whose limbic system and hormonal systems humans share, with horrific brutality made invisible in carnivory.

The Road's cannibals have abandoned the pretense of human exceptionalism amid the facts of a world where environmental devastation is complete and there can be no future for the human species, eating each other because there is nothing much else. Aside from other human beings and one barking dog (who quickly goes silent), there is absolutely nothing alive in *The Road*. The man and boy find wild foods only twice, and both times those food sources are remnants of a past living world, not forerunners of a regenerating, growing landscape. In the first case, they discover morel mushrooms, "a small colony of them, shrunken, dried and wrinkled" (40). Although they eat the mushrooms, they cannot grow the "small alien-looking things" (40) for a future meal: not only are the mushroom spores dead, but morels cannot be readily cultivated in even the best circumstances. In the second case, the man finds "hard and brown and shriveled" apples, "dry and almost tasteless" that he eats "seeds and all" (121) before searching what was once an orchard and finding more than he can carry. But the "black and gnarly stumps" (118) will not produce more apples, so like some regressive Johnny Appleseed he can only eat his desiccated

[18]   Paul Patton, "McCarthy's Fire," in *Styles of Extinction: Cormac McCarthy's The Road*, ed. Julian Murphet and Mark Steven (New York: Continuum Publishing, 2013), 142.
[19]   Arielle Zibrak, "Intolerance, A Survival Guide: Heteronormative Culture Formation in Cormac McCarthy's *The Road*," *Arizona Quarterly* 63, no. 3 (Autumn 2012): 119.

find with no chance to grow more. The cannibals have adapted to survive in ecocollapse, their behavior further quickening the inevitable end of the human species in a caloric pyramid scheme.

Thus, I argue that the father's insistence that cannibalism is wrong *no matter what* is an attempt to reinscribe old taboos that no longer function in a dead and dying world; he fails to recognize the dissolution of now-irrelevant dualistic frameworks that construct hierarchies of human exceptionalism. In *The Road*, the few human survivors are all scavengers of increasingly scarce foodstuffs:

> What are you eating.
> Whatever we can find.
> Whatever you can find.
> Yeah. (64)

Although the man and boy define themselves as "good guys" who do not eat human meat, the fact is that human and nonhuman flesh is often indistinguishable: "They passed a metal trashdump where someone had once tried to burn bodies. The charred meat and bones under the damp ash might have been anonymous save for the shapes of the skulls" (150). Meat is meat, and often the food they scavenge is assumed to be nonhuman despite its source's ambiguity. For example,

> In an old batboard smokehouse they found a ham gambreled up in a high corner. It looked like something fetched from a tomb, so dried and drawn. He cut into it with his knife. Deep red and salty meat inside. Rich and good. They fried it that night over their fire, thick slices of it, and put the slices to simmer with a tin of beans. (17)

How do they know the "ham" is not human flesh, it being like something "fetched from a tomb" where human bodies are stored after death? They cannot possibly, and the meat is further connected to cannibalism by the area's bloodcults' music heard in the night: "He woke in the dark and he thought that he'd heard bulldrums beating somewhere in the low dark hills. Then the wind shifted and there was just silence" (17). Later, porcine and human flesh are again made equivalent when the man discovers "a forty gallon castiron cauldron of the kind once used for rendering hogs" (109), now used to stew human flesh. Thus, despite trying to retain a binary of "good" and "bad" ways to satisfy hunger, in actuality, the man's physical need for food dissolves the differences between species when it is possible and necessary for him to do so. Unless the flesh is unquestionably human—indicated by human skulls, for example, or the newborn infant's carcass on a spit—it is proper food. All flesh is meat, and when there is nothing else to be found in a country "looted, ransacked, ravaged. Rifled of every crumb" (129), it is better not to question the origins of a protein source too carefully. Therefore, there is no way for the man to be so assured of his "goodness" in the false binary he constructs between cannibals and himself.

The astute boy recognizes the fluidity of his father's categorizations, expressing his concerns that they might eventually become cannibals:

> We wouldnt ever eat anybody, would we?
>
> No. Of course not.
>
> Even if we were starving?
>
> We're starving now.
>
> . . .
>
> But we wouldnt.
>
> No. We wouldnt.
>
> No matter what.
>
> No. No matter what.
>
> Because we're the good guys.
>
> Yes. (128–9)

The repetition of the question reveals that the boy is not fully convinced by his father's assurances. The boy's consternation about the contesting distinctions between physical survival and psychological revulsion arises in the figure of the cannibal, in the dual fears of cannibalism exposed here: how to avoid becoming cannibal directly or by being incorporated into the body of a cannibal as food.

Because the father ignores the issue of their becoming cannibal inadvertently (by accidentally eating human flesh) or purposefully (by eating found human meat), the primary fear these characters express is of becoming food for cannibals. Thus, the most agonizing moments in the novel occur when the father and son encounter other people, even in the far distance, knowing how vulnerable they are as two of the few remaining life-forms in a completely collapsed ecosystem. Yet the novel reveals that the cannibals are not glorious warriors or demonized others but are similarly human animals, suffering and struggling to survive:

> When he looked back toward the road the first of them were already coming into view. God, he whispered. . . . They came shuffling through the ash casting their hooded heads from side to side. Some of them wearing canister masks. One in a biohazard suit. Stained and filthy. Slouching along with clubs in their hands, lengths of pipe. Coughing. (60)

The cannibals are not romanticized, not well fed, not living a much better existence for having a (purportedly) ready source of food. Instead, when trying to find a place to defecate, one of them stumbles upon the man and boy, and the holes in his belt

> marked the progress of his emaciation and the leather at one side had a lacquered look to it where he was used to stropping the blade of his knife. He stepped into the roadcut and he looked at the gun and he looked at the boy. Eyes collared in cups of grime and deeply sunk. Like an animal inside a skull looking out the eyeholes. He wore a beard that had been cut square across the bottom with shears and he had a tattoo of a bird on his neck done by someone with an illformed notion of their appearance. He was lean, wiry, rachitic. Dressed in a pair of filthy blue coveralls and a black billcap with the logo of some vanished enterprise embroidered across the front of it. (63)

Defecation presumes consumption, so the marauder is clearly eating something—although when confronted by the father, the marauder says they eat "whatever we can find" (64). Finding human flesh is no different than finding canned tomatoes to these survivors, a fact that might be discomforting but acknowledges the equation of human and nonhuman flesh in a world of scarcity. In fact, the only evidence that this group of road rats are cannibals is their consumption of the body of their dead comrade after he is killed by the father. They are cannibals but not murderers, at least not this time: "The truck people had camped in the road itself. They'd built a fire there and charred billets of wood lay stuck in the melted tar together with ash and bones. . . . Coming back he found the bones and the skin piled together with rocks over them. A pool of guts. He pushed at the bones with the toe of his shoe. They looked to have been boiled. No pieces of clothing" (70–1). In fact, there is no textual evidence that they do anything but eat what they find—in this case, a dead body, killed and abandoned by the father. The difference between eating human meat and killing someone to get it is one the father refuses to acknowledge here, insisting instead that his own goodness remains because his job is to keep the boy alive at any cost, except, apparently, if that cost means the boy knows they eat human flesh to do it.[20] Pre-collapse ideals of being "good guys" must always be maintained to give them a reason to continue on their journey as the father clings to the exceptionalist standards of a now-dead world.[21]

Even so, the mutable logic of speciation means that there are few distinctions between cannibalism of convenience and cannibalism by design within the structure of the absent referent because both forms of carnivory depend on the process of turning living beings into edible nourishment and both inherently incorporate cruelty toward another being in that process. For example, the father and son hide from another walking group of "bad guys" (92), this time with enslaved people who might perhaps also be a food source: "Behind them came wagons drawn by slaves in harness and piled with goods of war and after that the women, perhaps a dozen in number, some of them pregnant, and lastly a supplementary consort of catamites illclothed against the cold and fitted in dogcollars and yoked each to each" (92). The language here connects these objectified people with nonhuman animals, harnessed and pulling wagons or yoked together like oxen, wearing dog collars, not considered human but treated no worse or better than a chained veal calf or a raped sheep or any one of the millions of enslaved people and animals in the world today. As George Monbiot observes, "All pre-existing social codes soon collapse and are

---

[20]   Although readers cannot be entirely sure because they always find food (even if it is meat from a questionable source) before the decision to eat something definitively human must be made.

[21]   Inger-Anne Softing claims that "Even in the face of these direst of circumstances they have retained their consciences and moral sense and not been reduced to bestiality," proving that even readers fall prey to the easy oppositions the father constructs here between himself and other humans. See "Between Dystopia and Utopia: The Post-Apocalyptic Discourse of Cormac McCarthy's *The Road*," *English Studies* 94, no. 6 (2016): 710. Nels Anchor Christensen similarly argues that "You either eat people or you don't. Unlike in the sky, there is no gray in the morality of *The Road*. Good and bad are stitched starkly in black and white" (200) in "Facing the Weather," *ISLE: Interdisciplinary Studies in Literature and Environment* 21, no. 1 (Winter 2014): 192–204.

replaced with organized butchery, then chaotic, blundering horror. What else are the survivors to do? The only remaining resource is human."[22]

Human exceptionalism disintegrates completely in a later scene at the southern plantation house, where "human" is faceless meat, aligned with "object" and entirely without subjectivity. The man and boy, starving, discover a mansion where "chattel slaves had once trod those boards bearing food and drink on silver trays" (106) and they scavenge, discovering under a padlocked floorboard "naked people, male and female, all trying to hide, shielding their faces with their hands. On the mattress lay a man with his legs gone to the hip and the stumps of them blackened and burnt. The smell was hideous" (110).[23] These captured people are utterly objectified via the absent referent, transformed into flesh only: not human, not subject. These cannibals' brutal, callous removal of body parts while their meat source is still alive recalls the acute trauma of highly intelligent pigs, who suffer castration, tail docking, ear notching, and teeth clipping without anesthetic painkillers at hog lots, from which the majority of pork originates in the United States.[24] Furthermore, the naked people are not covering their exposed genitals but their *faces*. In Levinasian terms, "the face opens the primordial discourse whose first word is obligation,"[25] but here the possibility of shared looks is extinguished by a lack of autonomy within the process of the absent referent. The imprisoned bodies share more with nonhumans in experimental laboratories or slaughterhouses than with the people consuming their flesh. Although the scene is repulsive to readers because we identify with the captured people, the novel describes nothing not currently experienced by beings of many species in the world today. It is because readers privilege and identify with humans that the scenario is appalling, even as the process of the absent referent turns those humans into

---

[22] George Monbiot, "Civilization Ends with a Shutdown of Human Concern. Are We There Already?" *The Guardian*, October 30, 2007.

[23] Andrew Hoberek's valuable reading of this scene attends to the "region specific history" of the novel's setting, illustrating that "embedded in the word 'chattel' and in resonance of the ship's holds and the slippage from chattel to cattle, we can see the quite organized forms of cannibalism McCarthy depicts in the novel not as Hobbesian throwbacks but as perverse extensions of regional tradition" in "Cormac McCarthy and the Aesthetics of Exhaustion," *American Literary History* 23, no. 3 (July 2011): 489.

[24] See M. A. Sutherland, et al. Note also that in the United States, livestock are excluded from the federal Animal Welfare Act and the majority of state laws expressly exempt farm animals from anti-cruelty provisions.

[25] Emmanuel Levinas, *Totality and Infinity*, trans. A. Lingis (Pittsburgh, PA: Duquesne University Press, 1969), 201.

food for their cannibal captors in exactly the same way humans make invisible the suffering of animals on their own plates. Thus, at the end of *The Road* when the boy is found by a family with children and asks for assurance that they "dont eat people," the friendly man's response—"No. We dont eat people."—is meaningless except that he and the woman have apparently not killed their children (284). Not even the cannibals "eat people," having stripped the source of their meat from any notions of humanity. In a novel filled with half-eaten humans; sunken, sullen, and starving faces; a traumatized, blood-soaked child; a walking train of catamites; and numerous other horrors,[26] the father says that the good guys "keep trying. They dont give up" (137). But that is also what the "bad" guys do. They just survive differently, employing the same methods by which carnivores today transform nonhuman flesh into food to transform human flesh into the same type of nourishment. If, as Michael Titlestad argues, the road is "a site of diminution, on which survival is the best one can hope for,"[27] they are surviving too. Indeed, as Brent Ryan Bellamy illustrates, "The novel offers a certain expected journey—at once practical and spiritual—and instead offers up only the literal *road* rather than any kind of self-discovery or kinship."[28]

Especially when compared to the man and boy, the cannibals are the closest to flourishing that *The Road* offers readers: they demonstrate culture and art, the pinnacle of human expression. Whereas species value is often described in terms of culture so as to exclude nonhuman animals, here again the cannibals complicate things. The road rat's carefully trimmed beard and bird-like tattoo are artful demonstrations of identity unnecessary to mere biological survival, for instance. Likewise, the marchers mark themselves as part of a shared community, "all wearing red scarves at their necks. Red or orange, as close to red as they could find" carrying "spears of lances tasseled with ribbons" (91). The most revealing example, though, is the funerary practices of one group of cannibals:

> The wall beyond held a frieze of human heads, all faced alike, dried and caved with their taut grins and shrunken eyes. They wore gold rings in their

---

26   McCarthy, *The Road*, 110, 96, 74, 92.
27   Quoted in Andrew Tate, *Apocalyptic Fiction*, 89.
28   Brent Ryan Bellamy, "The Reproductive Imperative of *The Road*," *The Cormac McCarthy Journal* 16, no. 1 (2018): 44. Emphasis in original.

leather ears and in the wind their sparse and ratty hair twisted about on their skulls. The teeth in their sockets like dental molds, the crude tattoos etched in some homebrewed woad faded in the beggared sunlight. Spiders, swords, targets. A dragon. Runic slogans, creeds misspelled. Old scars with old motifs stitched along their borders. The heads not truncheoned shapeless had been flayed of their skins and the raw skulls painted and signed across the forehead in a scrawl and one white bone skull had the plate sutures etched carefully in ink like a blueprint for assembly. (90)

The tattoos are undoubtedly drawn after the ecocollapse with their misspellings and scrounged ink and indicate a culture created in the new world. More significant, however, are the funerary customs revealed in the placement and decoration of skulls: is this not respect for the dead, whose bodies probably also provided nourishment after death? As the father notes in a different context, "Where you've nothing else construct ceremonies out of the air and breathe upon them" (74). Ironically, then, funerary practices and painted art signal both the beginning and the end of the human species.

So, while the supposed "bad guys" practice community, art, music with their drumming, and other forms of culture, the father and the boy have little beyond the necessities of bare biological survival. "Good" no longer manifests "civilized." Examining the frequent use of "okay" in *The Road* Paul D. Knox argues that "Surviving the wasteland requires more than finding food and shelter; surviving the wasteland requires re-creating the communities that the apocalypse has erased—even if these communities will exist only in the imagination."[29] The father rejects all opportunities for communal kinship, even with his son. In contrast to the cannibals, the father and boy have no one else; when the boy seeks companionship with others, the father thwarts his efforts; and they achieve very little beyond a bare physical survival. Early in the novel, the boy "found some crayons and painted his facemask with fangs" (14) and he has books and toys (70) but is "too tired for reading" (10) and is described imaginatively playing only a handful of times: playing made-up card games (53), playing with a truck (60), playing checkers (153), and building a sand town to be destroyed by the tide (245). His father carves him a flute, and he

---

[29] Paul D. Knox, "'Okay Means Okay': Ideology and Survival in Cormac McCarthy's *The Road*," *The Explicator* 70, no. 2 (2012): 97.

creates "a formless music for the age to come. Or perhaps the last music on earth called up from out of the ashes of its ruin" (77).[30] The boy doesn't play it again:

> What happened to your flute?
>
> I threw it away.
>
> You threw it away?
>
> Yes.
>
> Okay.
>
> Okay. (159)

Their lives are bereft of joy, of companionship beyond each other, and of any connection to a shared sense of identity kinship beyond being "the good guys" and the amorphous "carrying the fire" phrase. Furthermore, their companionship is imbalanced and unsatisfactory to the boy, who accurately declares that his father never listens to him (211). If, within the structure of human exceptionalism, art and culture are exclusively "human" characteristics beyond the ordinary animal, the man does not enable a fulfilling camaraderie bursting with cultural attributes. As Arielle Zibrak points out, "The culture that the man creates for the boy is only applicable to a world in which they no longer live" because the father considers all other people potential "agents of death" rather than "avenues for survival or cultural reunification."[31] Before dying, the man tells the boy to "find the good guys" (278), but his consistent dehumanization of others means the boy has to fight the structures of fear established by the father in order to do so. Furthermore, what purpose any reunification serves in an ecocollapsed landscape is unclear except in the example of the cannibals, who will eat dead bodies and each other to extinction.

Because the new world ruptures the binary narratives of old taboos, mercy killings and suicide become reasonable choices to all except the father, who cannot accept that there is no future for his son. He illustrates the kind of attachment that Lauren Berlant theorizes in *Cruel Optimism*:

---

[30] Apparently, because the drumming is performed by the "bad guys," the father does not consider it music.

[31] Zibrak, "Intolerance," 108.

> Whatever the content of the attachment is, the continuity of its form provides something of the continuity of the subject's sense of what it means to keep on living on and to look forward to being in the world. . . . The fear is that the loss of the promising object/scene itself will defeat the capacity to have any hope about anything.[32]

Even as he is dying, the man clings to the boy as an object of hope. The boy's mother, in contrast, resolves that deciding when to become physically dead is the only agency she has left and kills herself; she has a more realistic perspective than the father does and thus might help us further flesh out the decision that Simpson's unnamed narrator makes by aborting her fetus, her "good luck" the mantra of a journey readers see developed in McCarthy's novel. In *The Road*, when the father tries to convince his wife that they are survivors, she exclaims, "What in God's name are you talking about? We're not survivors. We're the walking dead in a horror film" (55). Murder/suicide is the compassionate choice, to her understanding:

> You have two bullets and then what? You cant protect us. You say you would die for us but what good is that? I'd take him with me if it weren't for you. You know I would. It's the right thing to do. . . . Sooner or later they will catch us and they will kill us. They will rape me. They'll rape him. They are going to rape us and kill us and eat us and you wont face it. You'd rather wait for it to happen. But I cant. I cant. (56)

As Hannah Stark observes, the mother's absence in the novel "positions her as a failed mother," especially when contrasted with the woman at the end of the book, who is supposedly "a good mother not only for staying alive but also, the text explicitly tells us, for not eating her children."[33] However, being a "failed mother" in an ecocollapsed world is meaningless: the boy's mother simply decided not to participate, rejecting the premise: "They say that women dream of danger to those in their care and men of danger to themselves. But I dont dream at all" (57). When she commits suicide, she leaves the fate of the boy up to the father: can anyone say she is or is not a "good" mother for having done so?[34] Such category distinctions no longer apply.

---

[32] Lauren Berlant, *Cruel Optimism* (Durham, NC: Duke University Press, 2011), 24.
[33] Hannah Stark, "'All These Things He Saw and Did Not See': Witnessing the End of the World in Cormac McCarthy's *The Road*," *Critical Survey* 25, no. 2 (2013): 81–2.
[34] McCarthy attempts to do so, as Brent Ryan Bellamy details in "The Reproductive Imperative."

Images of dead babies further problematize what it means to be a "good" or "bad" parent by disputing moral taboos against neonaticide. These are worlds where nothing but babies can grow. Within the two stories described in "Diary" and *The Road*, the first image is Maia's baby, stuck, "died inside her" in "Diary" (Simpson 151). The second is the fetus wrapped in the "good blue shirt" (159), where there is little question that the narrator is doing a compassionate act by aborting her fetus, further emphasized when she leaves her best shirt as a funeral shroud. Hers are efforts of empathy in the chaotically ecocollapsing setting of the story. The third, a striking image, is the barbequed infant in *The Road*, and that is the most demanding scene. The man and boy first encounter "Three men and a woman. The woman walked with a waddling gait and as she approached he could see she was pregnant. . . . All of them wretched-looking beyond description" (195). A few days later, tantalizing smells of cooking meat tempt the man and boy toward a fire, where they discover "a charred human infant headless and gutted and blackening on the spit" (199), abandoned uneaten. To move past revulsion is to ask the tough question: what is really "wrong" here? It is not killing the newborn, because a quick death is a compassionate death in the ecocollapsed setting. It may be the absence of parental attachment, although attachment is complicated by the boy's mother, disappearing into the night after refusing to say goodbye where "the coldness of it was her final gift" (58), further problematized by the father's abandonment later in the novel. Instead, as my argument about carnivory and cannibalism makes explicit, the wrongness is the waste, precious nutrients forsaken when the man and boy scare the four people away from their fire and then do not eat the meat themselves, while simultaneously continuing with the pretense that they are "survivors" and "the good guys." Any notion of moral wrong is a residue of human exceptionalism.

Equally, the "goodness" of the father's parenting is in question because killing the young boy humanely would certainly protect him from the horrors he experiences traveling south with his father. The boy is in a constant state of emotional trauma: he sees captives held in a basement being slowly harvested for food; he is covered with brains and blood when the father shoots the road rat; he views a headless infant skewered and roasting over a firepit; and general terror, hunger, and stress leaves the young boy in a unremitting condition of dread.[35] When the father has only one bullet left, he finally admits to himself: "You will not face the truth. You will not" (68), the truth being that he is unable to protect his son from the evils of the world and he will not shoot him to save him from them. Jane Elliott reads the father's insistence on keeping his son alive as part of an "excruciating portrayal of the way in which suffering agency is forged from the apparently unbreakable links between interest and choice and choice and agency" because he cannot override his interest in his son's life even at the expense of his son's future suffering.[36] To the father, the boy always remains an object of cruel optimism in order "to guarantee the endurance of something, the survival of something, the flourishing of something, and above all the protection of the desire that made this object . . . powerful enough to have magnetized an attachment to it"[37] even as the father dies. Although the mother cannot know it when she opens her veins with a piece of obsidian (selflessly leaving the two remaining bullets for her husband and son), she was correct: the father does leave the boy alone and unprotected in an even worse world, still facing the same decision his mother made so many years before with no one to help him through it. As the father lies dying of a wound, exacerbated by a mysterious cough, exhaustion, and starvation, he refuses to take the boy with him when he begs to die too: "I cant. I cant hold my son dead in my arms. I thought I could but I cant" (279). As the mother expected, the "greater danger" to the father was his own. Instead of putting a bullet through his son's head, he leaves the boy to wander the ashy, barren, dangerous world alone. "You said you wouldn't ever leave me," the boy protests. "I know. I'm sorry" is the father's empty reply, not the certain "I will do what I promised. No matter what. I will not send you into the darkness alone" of a few days before (279, 248). Inger-Anne Softing argues that "by not killing him he sets his son free; the boy is no longer his father's custodian, he is his own keeper and his own destiny. He is an orphan and as such it could be

---

[35] Surprisingly, Ashley Kunsa sees the boy as evidence that the world will be recreated, that there is such a possibility: "The boy serves as an Adamic figure, a messiah not unlike Christ himself" (65), claiming there is "eloquent hope" in the novel (69) in " 'Maps of the World in Its Becoming': Post-Apocalyptic Naming in Cormac McCarthy's *The Road*," *Journal of Modern Literature* 33, no. 1 (Fall 2009): 57–74.

[36] Elliott, "Suffering Agency," 93. She also calls the father's decision "selfless," which I find befuddling.

[37] Berlant, *Cruel Optimism*, 48.

said that his ties to the past have been severed and that his direction is to the future,"[38] although that future is one of either suicide or extended suffering and trauma. Readers are left to ponder impossible questions: What does empathy mean? What are the obligations of love in this world? Would the mother's way not have been more humane, the last compassionate act of a vulnerable animal in an impossible world? Simpson's narrator's fetus, wrapped in her best blue shirt and securely buried, seems comparatively well-off.

Aside from the fact that in both "Diary of an Interesting Year" and *The Road* most or all other animals are dead, the vulnerability of simply living—and even then, at the level of mere mortal survival in an ecocollapsed world—erases any residual gap between species that structures human exceptionalism. Both women in these texts recognize "human" no longer exists, which motivates their decisions: to protect herself or her child from the vulnerability of rare biological existence in an ecocollapsed world "largely populated by men who would eat your children in front of your eyes" (McCarthy 181). The mother in *The Road* says, "My heart was ripped out of me the night he was born," and when she welcomes the "eternal nothingness" of death, her hope for that nothingness extends to the boy, her heart (57). As Bellamy demonstrates, the woman "emphasizes what will turn out to be the lesson of the novel when she says, 'there is no stand to take'; that is, the actions of the woman or the man will never be able to effect any change in the shape of the narrative present. She denies all imperatives but the mortal one."[39] Likewise, the narrator in "Diary" identifies that "There's no future now for any baby aboveground" (159). Both women choose no-nonsense practicality over now-irrelevant idealizations about human exceptionalism. In contrast, the father refuses to accept the truth of extinction: "There was yet a lingering odor of cows in the barn and he stood there thinking about cows and he realized they were extinct. Was that true? There could be a cow somewhere being fed and cared for. Could there? Fed what? Saved for what?" (McCarthy 120). Although the father can comprehend the absurdity of the cow surviving, he cannot accept that his son is not a precious exception. For him, his son's humanness excludes him from the reality of mass extinction, and by clinging to now-corrupt notions of

---

[38]   Softing, "Between Dystopia and Utopia," 712.
[39]   Bellamy, "The Reproductive Imperative," 43.

human exceptionalism and morality, he cannot execute his son either. He fails the boy, leaving his animal body vulnerable to an unforgiving death-world. By aborting her fetus, Simpson's narrator forgoes all ties to the future and, as she states, ensures she is "the end of the line" (Simpson 159), impervious to any additional vulnerabilities.

In contrast to the nothingness of death is the only potential future "life" these fictions provide, hinted at by the ragged, starving, old man in *The Road*, Ely. Ely passively bridges good and bad, eats whatever he is offered, even human meat, and otherwise docilely waits for death. Ely appears after a bizarre exchange between the boy and the man wherein they discuss their "long term goals" (160), and what Ely represents is the best-case scenario for the boy's optimum future, if temporary survival is the goal. The boy spots Ely first: "Papa, he whispered. The man looked up. A small figure distant on the road, bent and shuffling" (161). The father thinks, "It could be a decoy"—"it," not "he," marking Ely's object status. They follow to see if he turns around:

> The traveler was not one for looking back. They followed him for a while and then they overtook him. An old man, small and bent. He carried on his back an old army rucksack with a blanket roll tied across the top of it and he tapped along with a peeled stick for a cane. When he saw them he veered to the side of the road and turned and stood warily. He had a filthy towel tied under his jaw as if he suffered from toothache and even by their new world standards he smelled terrible. (161)

The boy wants to feed him and gives Ely a tin of fruit, and then invites the "starved and threadbare buddha" (168) to eat more in a conversation suggestive of the ambiguity of carnivory and cannibalism when Ely asks, "Eat what?" (166) and later says, "You don't want to know the things I've eaten" (172). Just like the boy passively accepts what the man provides him, Ely passively accepts whatever comes, somehow living on whatever "other people on the road" give him to eat (170), a monk without even an alms bowl. These "other people," who may or may not exist (there is some question of Ely's reliability), remind readers that the man's refusal to join another group or incorporate human others into his own circle is a choice, one not made out of absolute necessity. There are "communes," one from which the thief was outcast, for example (255), and the man resists every opportunity to join up with other people, a child, or even a dog. He seems to affirm Hannah Stark's claim that the man "embodies the characteristics of American individualism: self-reliance, resourcefulness, and independence,"[40] even though that exceptionalism fails when the father dies. What does the boy's life look like, then, should he survive to adulthood? If Ely is the measure, he will "live like an animal" and not admit even to himself the things he eats (172). He will live without the voice of his father in his head because "where men cant live gods fare no better" (172). He will wish he had died, much like the boy already wishes he could die because "When we're all gone at last then there'll be nobody here but death and his days will be numbered too. He'll be out in the road there with nothing to do and nobody to do it to. He'll say: where did everybody go? And that's how it will be. What's wrong with that?" (173). The specter of Death becomes the final witness to human extinction. If, as Kenneth Lincoln claims, *The Road* is "a survivor manual" for readers,[41] it is one that foregrounds agential death rather than ongoing flourishing life.

The abandoned boy with no meaningful future in a dead global ecosystem gives readers further hints of what the path ahead holds for the narrator in "Diary" as she heads north with her rucksack and gun. The road will be a desolate one, a melted, debris-littered slab of asphalt that presents some of the most terrifying moments to the characters who travel it. Maybe she will see human bodies on the road itself, "figures half mired in the blacktop, clutching themselves, mouths howling" (McCarthy 190). Perhaps like the boy and his father she will hide in the brush or woods away from the road, hoping no one discovers her, eating whatever she can scavenge. In the last pages of the novel, after the father dies and the boy mourns, though, the road calls him back out: "He stayed three days and then he walked out to the road and he looked down the road and he looked back the way they had come. Someone was coming. He started to turn and go back into the woods but he didnt. He just stood in the road and waited, the pistol in his hand" (281). The road can bring death or another temporary reprieve, he knows not which. One is just a postponement of the other: there is no future in a destroyed global

---

40   Stark, "All These Things," 81.
41   Kenneth Lincoln, *Cormac McCarthy* (New York: Palgrave, 2009), 165.

habitat, no good or bad guys, no meaningful life to experience. Simpson and McCarthy allow no false hope in these ecocollapse fictions: there is just obliteration, immanent human extinction, and the concomitant reframing of ethical, social, and species boundaries that enable—at best—only a temporary material existence.

Thus, instead of a fantasy future world where humans live in primitive harmony with nature and one another, these realistic ecocollapse narratives demand a radical questioning of the desire for that world. Simpson's insistence on upturning class as a factor of survival, for instance, hints at the possibility that marginalized and poor communities might also have the knowledge to survive in the short term because they are granted less access to knowledge resources and technology amid the innumerable systemic injustices they face.[42] This implication is unrealistic. Global warming is immediately disastrous for populations in the earth's mid-latitudes and thus is even more likely to have a disproportionately negative impact on the poorest parts of the world, as refugee movements already demonstrate. The poorest and most marginalized, in other words, are already facing ecocollapses. According to Elizabeth Rush in *Rising: Dispatches from the New American Shore*, "The reality is that many living on climate change's front lines are low- to working-class people and communities of color, whose relationships with the more-than-human world regularly go unaccounted for in the 'official story' of environmentalism we tell in this country."[43] Western civilization denies the environmental experience that millions of people live every day where the internet, supermarkets, and condoms are unavailable to many, and Simpson's story reveals the lie told by the generic convention of climate change fiction, which longs for a romanticized, simplified, pastoral recreation of society and frequently elides harsh realities about who might actually survive.

With these connections to McCarthy's *The Road*, Simpson's "Diary of an Interesting Year" challenges the boundaries of typical climate fiction and leaves readers with an even more complicated and ambiguous conclusion than the controversial ending of McCarthy's novel, which is interpreted as implying "an

---

[42]   See Rob Nixon, *Slow Violence and the Environmentalism of the Poor* (Cambridge, MA: Harvard University Press, 2011).
[43]   Quoted in Emily Raboteau, "Lessons in Survival," *The New York Review of Books*, November 21, 2019, 13.

indistinct but expanding future" wherein "the journey, it is implied, continues for the boy" according to Tate (96); or, even more hopeful, where "the burned out landscape, strangely, is a new if unlikely Eden" according to Kunsa (62) as two examples of the deep desire to find a livable future for the human species I have shown does not exist in the novel. To put it more explicitly, "Diary" defers human extinction because the narrative ends with the diary's burial in a hole in the ground, yet Simpson replaces the patriarchal worldview typically seen in this genre with a feminist one that confronts the stereotypes of vulnerability and oppression developed within it to reveal the possibility of both resistance and capitulation. Simpson's narrator outwits and murders her captor, appropriating his weapon and supplies and thus better insuring her own (albeit temporary) survival as she refuses to be submissive to her own biology. She quickly adapts into a single-minded, self-centered, and liberated opportunist, leaving any passive acceptance of her vulnerability in the hole she digs for her dead fetus and diary. Rather than a birth symbolizing recreation and reproductive futurity, an aborted fetus and the last page of the journal symbolize the extinction of the human species and of storytelling itself.

The troubling consequences of autonomous individualism are also made clear: survival for the solitary individual is neither possible nor desirable, since without meaningful, engaged community few survive—or want to—for long. By the end of her journal, she is newly equipped with all that she has learned during her remarkable journey, not the least of which is a strong awareness of her own post-technological, post-cultural abilities as a human animal in a denatured environment. Unlike the figures characterized in much post-apocalyptic literature, then, the narrator in Simpson's story simultaneously demonstrates the effects of human exceptionalism's narcissistic tendencies even as it demands she—and readers—witness the consequences of human arrogance, scientific hubris, individualism, and technology gone amuck. We have no doubt that she can turn the gun on herself should her tomorrow be one not worth living. There will thus be no recreation of humanity. She is just reporting, giving witness to an early stage of humanity's inevitable extinction. Taken together, then, these fictions help us imagine what humanity's destruction might look like, those of us who are parents especially cognizant that it is our children who will suffer the greatest consequences of climate change. Captivatingly, though, McCarthy alludes to what might come next, which species might flourish in the ecocollapsed world: the "life in the deep" (219) of the "alien sea" (215), perhaps? Some scientists think so, and we will ponder these questions more closely in Chapter 5. But first, in the next chapter I examine another literary post-apocalyptic trope, the population-reducing pandemic, exploring another realistic novel of ecocollapse that nonetheless leaves no hope for human species regeneration despite reduced competition for resources.

4

Bearing Witness: Narrating Human Extinction in *The Dog Stars*

The final paragraph of Cormac McCarthy's *The Road* seems out of place. It is one that readers and scholars have debated since the novel's publication: is it intended to display hope? Redemption? Or is it a memory of what is lost?

> Once there were brook trout in the streams in the mountains. You could see them standing in the amber current where the white edges of their fins wimpled softly in the flow. They smelled of moss in your hand. Polished and muscular and torsional. On their backs were vermiculate patterns that were maps of the world in its becoming. Maps and mazes. Of a thing which could not be put back. Not be made right again. In the deep glens where they lived all things were older than man and they hummed of mystery.[1]

Peter Heller's protagonist Hig in the novel *The Dog Stars* (2012) reiterates this now-famous image of trout to make explicit that there is no return from global ecocollapse:

> If I ever woke up crying in the middle of a dream, and I'm not saying I did, it's because the trout are gone every one. Brookies, rainbows, browns, cutthroats, cutbows, every one.
>
> The tiger left, the elephant, the apes, the baboon, the cheetah. The titmouse, the frigate bird, the pelican (gray), the whale (gray), the collared dove. Sad but. Didn't cry until the last trout swam upriver looking for maybe cooler water.[2]

---

[1] Cormac McCarthy, *The Road* (New York: Vintage Books, 2006), 286–7. Subsequent citations appear parenthetically in the text.
[2] Peter Heller, *The Dog Stars* (New York: Vintage Books, 2012), 3. Subsequent citations appear parenthetically in the text.

Unlike in *The Road*, where the apocalypse leaves the human population largely intact to compete for diminished resources, in *The Dog Stars* a disease first depopulates the earth of people alongside (and perhaps exacerbated by) warming weather patterns and the mass extinction of other species. In that sense, then, the novel describes a scenario where the depopulation event, although quick and effective, leaves human survivors with a different kind of struggle than is apparent in *The Road*'s absolute destruction of a livable world. Nonetheless, Heller's novel explores the psychological effects of loss and individual adaptations to the breakdowns of human civilization and concomitant cultural transformations. Hig clings to the past in eerily similar ways to the man in *The Road*: "He calls his father. He calls his mother. They are gone for years only a hum now on the line but still he calls" (Heller 30). Likewise, in *The Road*, the man "picked up the phone and dialed the number of his father's house in that long ago" (McCarthy 7). Both protagonists reveal the futility of "survival," going through the motions of the past while trying to determine what it means to live in a post-apocalyptic world. Indeed, as Walter Benjamin observes in "Critique of Violence," "The proposition that existence stands higher than a just existence is false and ignominious if existence is to mean nothing other than mere life."[3] Whereas McCarthy's *The Road* approaches an exploration of "mere life" through the man's denial and a retention of false structures of human exceptionalism, Heller's *The Dog Stars* reveals the challenges of a "just existence" from a different angle. This chapter interrogates the intersections of ecocollapse, disease, and the disintegration of humanity in *The Dog Stars*, as problematized alongside the worldviews uncovered in *The Road*, "Diary of an Interesting Year," and Yann Martel's *Life of Pi*, and compared to another post-pandemic climate change scenario fictionalized in Emily St. John Mandel's *Station Eleven* (2014). Part of the answer to the question of what it means to be human rests in how characters fight the tendency to focus only on their own short-term physical survival. *The Dog Stars*, like *The Road*, tries to establish moral clarity through explicit binaries of "Nice"/"Not Nice," in which survival of the fittest (whatever that might mean in each context)

---

[3]   Walter Benjamin, "Critique of Violence," in *Selected Writings: 1913–1926 Volume 1*, ed. and trans. Marcus Paul Bullock, Michael William Jennings, and Howard Eiland (Boston, MA: Harvard University Press, 1996), 251.

means doing whatever needs done to remain alive. Here, those survivors who retain the most of their "humanity" are the ones who complicate the instinct for self-preservation at any price, overlapping and interweaving various dichotomous structures of being. Human exceptionalism breaks down in *The Dog Stars*: Hig records his species' extinction *as the last witness*, signified in part by a failure of reproductive futurity. Thus, rather than portraying false hope for species regeneration, Hig models a way out of learned hopelessness in the face of catastrophic pandemical ecocollapse.

The Dog Stars is narrated by Hig, a forty-year-old pilot who lives at an abandoned airport with his dog, Jasper, near another survivor named Bangley, an older man who maintains an arsenal of "all kinds of shit" (8) and thus likely had military experience before a flu and subsequent blood disease killed all but 1 percent of humans. Hig's wife Melissa dies before the narration begins but is resurrected in flashbacks where we learn that Hig empathetically euthanized her: "She had dysentery-like nausea and diarrhea and her lungs were filling up like pneumonia which was terrifying. In the end she just wanted it to be over. Pillow, she whispered to me" (64). Hig, in contrast to the father in *The Road*, recognizes that there are many kinds of suffering and survival: death can be a release. For most of the novel, a series of remembrances written a decade after the pandemic, Hig and Bangley work together to patrol and defend the eight miles of open ground between the surrounding mountains and the small country airport where they live. "I have the plane, I am the eyes, he has the guns, he is the muscle," Hig tells us (6). The depopulation event reduces human interactions, but Bangley shoots anyone who comes inside their perimeter, even once a young girl, although "after the second summer they tapered off, like turning off a faucet, drip drip. One visitor a season maybe, then none. Not for almost a year, then a band of four desperados that almost cleaned our clock. That's when I started flying regular like a job" (11). Heller paints a Waldenesque picture of the post-pandemic world: the characters hunt, grow and gather food, have relatively safe living conditions, and readily handle any attacks on their territory, called "Erie." When Hig finally flies away on an exploration quest, what pushes him away from Bangley and their territory is not physical survival (in contrast to the man and boy in *The Road*, who will not last the winter if they do not keep moving) but a longing for greater companionship, a man's voice heard on the radio spurring him on. "I cannot live like this," he says. "Cannot live at all not really. What was I doing? Nine years of pretending" (162). The death of his beloved dog Jasper is the catalyst; Hig goes searching for people past his plane's fuel capacity and discovers Pop and Cima, whom he brings back to the airport hangar to live with him and Bangley after the three escape a dangerous trap at the Grand Junction airport. But this novel does not have a happy ending. Like McCarthy's *The Road*, there is no hope for a rebirth of civilization, despite Jennifer Reese's claim that the most disturbing part of the novel may be "that his story is not in the end depressing."[4] Instead, I reveal that Heller's novel explores grief, agency, and compassion while Hig documents the human species going extinct, individual by individual, in a rapidly warming world, acknowledging the truth as the last survivor that "life and death lived inside each other" (68). A careful reading demonstrates that there is no clear demarcation between Nice and Not Nice, and Hig is left alone at the end, having "survived" by being both.

Like so many other post-apocalyptic novels, *The Dog Stars* maintains a focus on these issues by killing 99 percent of the human population with a deadly flu[5] followed by a blood disease but problematizes the traditional recreation of society by intertwining disease, violence, and climate change. The flu has mysterious origins, although Cima, a public health epidemiologist in New York City before the pandemic, says it was rumored to be the US government's creation of a genetically modified superbug as part of its biological warfare research that was accidentally released into the water supply during a plane crash. Because the high fever damaged survivors' organs, life expectancy is likely no older than 50, and many who survived the flu contracted the blood disease soon after: "Something like AIDS I think, maybe more contagious. The [Mennonite] kids were born with it and it makes them all sick and weak and every year some die" (7). Cima bruises easily and says of her fragility that "it's the result of damage to my blood vessels. I hemorrhage quite easily. My muscles get very sore as well. A type of fibromyalgia. You see I contracted the flu. I barely survived. One result of the prolonged fever was the systemic inflammation that resulted in these conditions" (208). She cannot have sex without injury,

4   Jennifer Reese, "'Dog Stars' Dwells on the Upside of Apocalypse," review of *The Dog Stars*, by Peter Heller, *NPR Books*, August 7, 2012.
5   See works by Claire P. Curtis, Andrew Tate, and Adam Trexler for more about the generic conventionality of the pandemic trope.

precluding any children from being born to her and Hig, effectively halting any chance of their group's future flourishing. The novel further suggests that the blood disease causes an autoimmune response "speeded by a breakdown in the body's ability to make its own vitamin D. Really a curious mechanism" (316), but, as I develop below, the intertwined complications of people, place, and disease make potential treatment largely irrelevant in a warming world.

Infectious disease creates a fascinating ontological status, the microscopic viral and bacterial infestations of our human selves an imbrication with nonhuman agency, frighteningly intimate with our fleshy bodies yet existing largely beyond our self-awareness. This intimacy is one form of the trans-corporeality that Stacy Alaimo theorizes in *Bodily Natures* when she demands "a recognition not just that everything is interconnected but that humans are the very stuff of the material, emergent world."[6] After Hurricane Katrina, the Centers for Disease Control concluded that climate change requires enhanced infectious disease surveillance and outbreak response preparation; more than a decade later, climate scientists and medical professionals sound even louder alarms about the effects of climate change to the global distribution and prevalence of vector-borne, airborne, direct-contact, and fluid-transmitted infectious disease.[7] A 2018 report from the Centers for Disease Control and Prevention revealed a staggering threefold increase between 2004 and 2016 in the United States alone of reported cases of vector-borne diseases (those transmitted by mosquitoes, lice, ticks, and other blood-feeding insects) and nine new pathogens. Climate-sensitive diseases like malaria, dengue fever, West Nile virus, cholera, and Lyme disease are expected to further worsen as higher temperatures and more extreme weather events wrack the globe. Yet these are only the known diseases: long-dormant bacteria and viruses, formerly trapped in glacial ice and permafrost, are exposed as ice sheets melt and ground temperatures increase. In 2005, a bacterium encased in a frozen pond for 32,000 years animated once the ice melted. Two years later, scientists managed to revive an eight-million-year-old bacterium that had

---

[6] Stacy Alaimo, *Bodily Natures: Science, Environment, and the Material Self* (Bloomington: Indiana University Press, 2010), 20. See also Lynn Margulis's *Symbiotic Planet* (1998) and Donna Haraway's *The Companion Species Manifesto* (2003) as crucial works that uncover the interwoven aspects of human biology with that of other species.

[7] The World Health Organization's warning is available at who.int/globalchange/summary/en/index5.html.

been lying dormant in Antarctic ice. Modern humans have no immunological defense against such reawakened infectious potential.[8] David Wallace-Wells points out that "what concerns epidemiologists more than ancient diseases are existing scourges relocated, rewired, or even re-evolved by warming" because "global warming will scramble ecosystems [and] help disease trespass [geographical] limits."[9] Many zoonotic pathogens threaten human populations, as demonstrated by recent outbreaks of Avian Influenza, Ebola, Middle East Respiratory Syndrome, Zika, and the Covid-19 global pandemic.[10]

In *The Dog Stars*, pandemic is spread by a downed plane, evoking the climate change consequences and disease risks of global air travel made ironic by Hig's position as a pilot and his continued dependence on flight. In this sense, *The Dog Stars* is similar to Mandel's *Station Eleven*, which also clears the way for survivors' existential challenges by implementing a pandemic first. Andrew Tate observes that "one of the reasons the world dies so quickly in *Station Eleven* is because of its relentless mobility and the ordinary miracle of air travel: people travel across the globe in hours and the virus, horribly resistant to treatment, goes with them."[11] Although *The Dog Stars* is narrated exclusively by Hig and interwoven with flashbacks and memories of conversations, *Station Eleven* foregrounds multiple narrative voices to "explore many different modalities of life in light of the near-extinction of the species."[12] Each narrator's experience fleshes out the various ways in which, to quote *Station Eleven*'s repeated refrains, "Survival is insufficient" and "I regret nothing." As Tate puts it, the novel "appears to show more faith in the sparks of ingenuity that create civilizations," describing it as "an ambitious . . . exploration of the human capacity to create and to pursue meaning via art, story and shared

---

[8] Bacteria trapped in small fluid pockets for more than four million years in a cave in Northern Mexico revived and began multiplying and, when tested, showed resistance to eighteen types of antibiotics, including drugs of last resort. See Jasmin Fox-Skelly, "There Are Diseases Hidden in Ice, and They Are Waking Up," *BBC Earth*, May 4, 2017.

[9] David Wallace-Wells, *The Uninhabitable Earth: Life after Warming* (New York: Tim Duggan Books, 2019), 110, 111.

[10] The novel coronavirus 2019 pandemic has killed hundreds of thousands worldwide and is yet ongoing as I prepare this manuscript in June 2020 under a "stay at home" order. Whatever the outcome of this disease, social, political, economic, and environmental structures will never be the same.

[11] Andrew Tate, *Apocalyptic Fiction* (New York: Bloomsbury, 2017), 133. Subsequent citations appear parenthetically in the text.

[12] Pieter Vermeulen, "Beauty That Must Die: *Station Eleven*, Climate Change Fiction, and the Life of Form," *Studies in the Novel* 50, no. 1 (Spring 2018): 11.

community" (133). The Travelling Symphony performs Shakespeare's plays, for example, their "quixotic endeavours . . . emblematic of a refusal to capitulate to despair or aggressive rejection of community" (135). The happy ending of *Station Eleven* is full of promise: society is recreated, and there is promise of an even better future signaled by one character's admission that "there were moments when he was overcome by his good fortune at having found this place, this tranquility, this woman, *at having lived to see a time worth living in*."[13] The novel ends in "this awakening world" (332), distant "streets . . . lit up with electricity" (311) in which a temporarily slowed but otherwise familiar life continues. As Tate argues, "The novel takes the risk of believing that an ethical, cooperative version of society might be achievable" (Tate 137), the utopian vision so common in climate fiction's generic conventions. Because *Station Eleven* does not dare contemplate a complete human species extinction event, it excludes itself from equal consideration within the category of ecocollapse extinction fiction I interrogate here even though the prominence of finding community is in some ways analogous to Hig's motivations in *The Dog Stars*.

Rather than a depopulated-but-expanding future for fewer human survivors to navigate, *The Dog Stars* constructs a version of post-pandemic where, despite disease risk, the social lifeworld defines meaningful life as it does in *Station Eleven*, but no community permanently forms. The importance of companionship in Hig's ecocollapsed world bears closer scrutiny because seeking out other people goes against the instinct for self-preservation from the place of safety and material security seen in *The Dog Stars*. The novel constructs foils of Hig (a poetic idealist) and Bangley (a militaristic realist). Hig aspires to something more than mere survival, which is why he visits the sick Mennonites in their commune (all infected with "the Blood"), hesitates before killing (but does so), and ponders the voice he heard on the radio (maybe life is less terrible elsewhere). Bangley, in contrast, is quick to kill to protect the resources that he and Hig have accumulated, ridicules Hig for risking infection by visiting the Mennonites, and is happy to stay put in their compound. Bangley exists as a living embodiment of a "shoot first, ask questions later" philosophy except that he does not even ask questions

---

[13] Emily St. John Mandel, *Station Eleven* (New York: Vintage Press, 2014), 270 [my emphasis]. Subsequent citations appear parenthetically in the text.

because questions are from the before-time, before the Not Nice. "Old rules are done Hig," Bangley says. "Went the way of the woodpecker. Gone with the glaciers and the government. New world now. New world new rules" (43).[14] Hig manages because he has his dog Jasper and he can fly his plane, escaping the boundaries of earth where most of humanity has disintegrated into little pockets of resistance to one another: "I am the one flying over all of it looking down. Nothing can touch me" (50). Hig helps the Mennonite commune because doing so helps him feel like himself Before. At stake here is the question of who will be allowed in the small ordered society they have created. Bangley justifies a policy of exclusion based on the grounds of safety (and thus raises the question: if Bangley had not been so severely injured when Hig returned with Cima and Pops, what form would their welcome have taken?). Hig and Bangley have differing responses to the ethical problem of where to draw the circle of moral obligation: Hig wants to base the decision on the supposed-intruders' behaviors—a relational ontology—while Bangley decides instead to use their territory perimeter to mark an enclosed system, the lifeboat ethics identified by Janet Fiskio.[15] They seem to disagree on the scope of *who* and *what* is worthy of concern.

Accordingly, Hig's relationship with his dog Jasper enables a cross-species "worthiness" that evades Bangley's rules, allows an outlet for his compassion, and keeps him from suicide (14), an imbrication of human and nonhuman agency. Jasper was a puppy raised in Hig's former life with his wife Melissa, a blue heeler mix "with a great nose" (9), "son of Daisy" (7), who "still curls against my legs, still dreams in whimpers, still trembles under his own blanket, but I think he is mostly deaf now and useless as an alarm, which we will never let on to Bangley" (11). Jasper provides an occasion for rethinking human entitlement in the novel and exposes a great deal of denial on Hig's part. He refuses to think of Jasper's age in dog years; by doing so, he would have to face not just the death of his beloved canine companion but also the loss of the last fragment of his former world and the relationships it included.

[14] These are hardly "new rules." Bangley's military-style policies suggestively parallel those illuminated by Ben De Bruyn regarding governmental scenario planning for anticipated resource wars resulting from climate change, which is intriguing given Bangley's unspecified military experience. See "The Hot War: Climate, Security, Fiction," *Studies in the Novel* 50, no. 1 (Spring 2018): 43–67.
[15] Janet Fiskio, "Apocalypse and Ecotopia: Narratives in Global Climate Change Discourse," *Race, Gender & Class* 19, nos. 1–2 (2012): 12–36.

Jasper is functionally his child with Melissa. Furthermore, Jasper reaffirms Hig's own precarious hold on Niceness because "Jasper can't stomach Bangley unless it's like an emergency visitor situation in which case he keeps his trap shut, he's a team player" (14), identifying Bangley as a bad goose like the ones he would chase at the park, pre-flu. When Hig realizes Jasper died in his sleep, the passage's language stalls and starts and stalls, words failing—as they inevitably must—to capture the real experience of death and grief: "Jasper. Little brother. My heart. I'll start a fire. Put sticks over moss and start. I'll cook the last two fish. I'll eat one. I'll. . . . He is the only one now. The only sight. Which. Tomorrow I'll. I don't know" (108). Jasper's companionship connects Hig to the last bit of recursive mutual care. As Hig recognizes about himself, it is unclear "whether you are a good man or a bad man, or just a pretty good man in a fucked up world" (166), and the emotionally charged, interrupted fragments describing Jasper's death unsettle the structuring of such articulations with humanity and compassion, asking readers to ponder what it means to lose those connections within various speculative "survival" enculturations.

Perhaps that leaves Bangley as representative of a new version of morality, conceivably even a godlike one: Bangley *seems* always present, even at a distance; he sees and knows things that Hig does not. Hig describes him reverently: Bangley is unfailing, unhesitant, generous, above and beyond. When he is flying alone, Hig hears Bangley's voice in his head, like a new map to guide the pilot. Hig and Bangley choose different shelters in the airport community where they live, and it is revealed that both their choices are strategic but utterly different. Hig selects a house, but it is only a decoy: he really lives in the airplane hangar and sleeps outside, refusing on some level to admit that the world has changed forever. He cannot relinquish the past: "Maybe the provisional nature of eating in what's essentially a mechanic's garage makes me feel like none of this is permanent. Part of why I don't live in a house. Like living in a hangar, sleeping outside, I can pretend there's a house somewhere else, with someone in it, someone to go back to" (31). In contrast, Bangley moves into one of the large houses in the airport community from which he can see most of their territory, adamant that the past is gone forever and their current world is all that matters. Near the end of the novel, Hig discovers that Bangley has a nearly omniscient view:

He could see just about everything: over the low berm across the runway where I slept with Jasper, right to the dumpster we had dragged away from my house, my house that was a decoy. He could see the porch and front door of that house, down along the line of rusted plane hulks, two sides of the FBO building, the doorway to my hangar. Not much he could not cover from here, which is of course why he had chosen it. . . . And I felt standing there rising up in me the revulsion and admiration and I have to say—what? Love, maybe, that I had grown to feel for that certain fucked up individual. (304–5)

"Fucked up Bangley" presents an affect of enjoying himself, saying, "We are like kings Hig. It took the end of the world" (66). His choice of house affirms his attitude that he has accepted the present, although there are also suggestive moments of silence when Hig asks Bangley about his past, and late in the novel readers discover that Bangley had left everything in place upstairs in the house, "preserved like a room in one of those historic museums" (303). The contrast is not a simple one, then, although Heller writes them as foils. But careful readers note that Hig has an omniscient perspective too, just from a different angle. He has a distant but perceptive view of the ecocollapsed earth from the air:

He asked me that once: how do I know. How do I *know* someone is not inside our perimeter, in all that empty country, hiding, waiting to attack us? But [the] thing is I can see a lot. Not like the back of my hand, too simple, but like a book I have read and reread too many times to count, maybe like the Bible for some folks of old. I would know. A sentence out of place. A gap. Two periods where there should be one. I know. (7)

Their different viewpoints—the micro for Bangley, who can see everything moving near their compound, and the macro for Hig, who sees everything globally from the air—are a metaphor for their different philosophies as they experience apocalypse and extinction, yet those philosophies become thoroughly entangled in Hig's mind.

The superficial contrast between Hig and Bangley encourages readers to imagine what kind of person they would be at the end of the world. What does it mean to be a human survivor? When does one's humanity cease to exist? In Hig's self-image, Bangley is everything he is not. Hig describes Bangley as "My only neighbor. What can I say to Bangley. He has saved my bacon more times. Saving my bacon is his job. I have the plane, I am the eyes, he has the guns, he is the muscle. He knows I know he knows: he can't fly, I don't have the stomach for killing. Any other way probably just be one of us. Or none" (6). We learn that in fact Hig has the capacity to kill and has done so before, but he wants it to be a different kind of killing than what Bangley does: he wants it to be self-justified. Yet Hig talks to himself in Bangley's voice, especially when he is in danger: "I could hear Bangley's words like some kind of telepathic transmission" (131). When Hig is attacked by a large group of people in the woods, Bangley is right there with him, telling him what to do and when to do it. When Hig is about to kill his pursuers and Bangley tells him to "have fun," his thought process changes from fear to pleasure:

> Such a weird thing to say: Have fun. But the fucker meant it, that was the thing. It did something to my head. I was amped. Balanced the rifle on the deer hide, took the Glock out of the paddle holster on my belt and racked it, lay it on the fur to the right. Two feet over. Shook the red plastic bullet holders out of the box and worked each bullet out and lay it on the fur to the right of the rifle point forward, so I could thumb them in without changing their direction. My hands were shaking a little. Just a little. *Have fun.* Kind of changed everything. *You got exactly nothing to lose Hig.* That's what I told myself. So have fun. (130)

But there is something for Hig to lose, in his own self-image and rationalizations: his compassion and empathy. Such judgments, in the words of Steven Lukes, are "formulated in ways calculated to give moral values an objectivity they do not possess."[16] To stave off becoming too much like Bangley, who seems to enjoy picking off attackers (even when they are children), Hig leaves to find more survivors. Yet Bangley goes with him, in his head, two halves of the same Nice/Not Nice truth that exists in everyone, an imbrication of the false dichotomy. Bangley amplifies all the characteristics and behaviors that make Hig uneasy about himself.

As the narrator of the novel, Hig's rationalizations of his own goodness function to make invisible how he compartmentalizes killing in general. For example, Hig claims, "I kill deer. I have no problem killing deer. Dressing,

---

16 Steven Lukes, *Moral Relativism* (London: Picador, 2008), 60.

butchering, eating" (41), and recalls how he "loved to hunt" with his Uncle Pete and that "even as a boy, the killing part was my least favorite" (42). It is hard to separate the killing from every other aspect of hunting, although Hig tries to do so:

> I adored it all, and it seemed I didn't have any problem putting the cow elk in my sights, but the way she stumbled over the rockfall when I shot, tripping forward and somersaulting over her own neck, and the way her eye shone up at me and she scrabbled her useless legs sideways over the rocks before I shot again right into the head in a panic, and the life went out of her eye and her legs, and then the way when I dressed her the blood spilled onto the frozen ground and mixed pink with warm milk from her still feeding teats—
>
> Didn't like it. Did it every year for years afterward and loved it all including having elk in the freezer, but not that. Didn't even like to kill a bug. (43)

This passage's graphic description exposes Hig's rationalizations of his own complex morality. It is difficult to reconcile his adoration of the entirety of the hunting experience to everything except the killing, which is central to the hunt itself and is a key factor toward his physical survival in the post-pandemic ecocollapsed environment. Bangley convinces Hig that they must shoot to kill anyone they encounter without negotiation; likewise, the deer and rabbits are killed, no negotiation. Hig manipulates his self-image and ends up justifying to himself, and thus to readers, his actions through his introspection and dilemma, although the novel shows he readily puts both humans and nonhumans in his rifle sights and pulls the trigger. His is a kind of Humean post-hoc moral reasoning, his rationalizations "largely driven by moral emotions such as gratitude, shame, embarrassment, contempt, and perhaps most importantly, disgust. Moral reasoning . . . serves to justify our moral beliefs and actions, which are in fact caused by unconscious intuitive processes."[17] As Miranda puts it in *Station Eleven*, "no one ever thinks they're awful, even people who actually are. It's some sort of survival mechanism" (Mandel 106).

Even without a massive catastrophic event, individuals are forced throughout their lives to deal with the effects of the kinds of loss and moral culpability that

---

[17]   Ibid., 47.

Hig struggles with in this novel: those suffering can choose to escape life in death, choose to live their lives vulnerably, finding beauty *despite*, or they can lived closed off to the outside of self. In Mandel's *Station Eleven*, for example, the fact that violence and horror *always* exist is most explicitly seen in the character of Frank, Jeevan's brother. Frank, formerly a journalist for Reuters, was shot on assignment in Libya, an interweaving of events Jevon describes while remembering a past before Frank became dependent on a wheelchair:

> The bullet that would sever his spinal cord still twenty-five years away but already approaching: a woman giving birth to a child who will someday pull the trigger on a gun, a designer sketching the weapon or its precursor, a dictator making a decision that will spark in the fullness of time into the conflagration that Frank will go overseas to cover for Reuters, the pieces of a pattern drifting closer together. (Mandel 191)

The entanglement of traumas implied here includes not only Frank's but that of a mother, whose child turns to violence; a grown child becoming a murderer; the political and social upheaval that lead to violent action; and the militarization of everyday life. The gunshots Jeevan fears, the "lawless world" (191) he imagines outside of the apartment has always existed somewhere. Frank knows this truth intimately, telling Jeevan, "I spent a lot of time thinking about civilization. What it means and what I value in it. I remember thinking that I never wanted to see a war zone again, as long as I live. I still don't. . . . I think there's just survival out there, Jeevan" (183). Rather than mere survival, Frank chooses suicide, freeing Jeevan to leave the apartment alone.

In contrast to Jeevan's search for resources, Hig goes on a quest as part of his denial of reality, a temporary escape. Although Yann Martel's *Life of Pi* tries to teach us that "animals don't escape *to somewhere* but *from something*: something within their territory has frightened them—the intrusion of an enemy, the assault of a dominant animal, a startling noise— and sets off a flight reaction" (Martel 41), we saw in Chapter 2 how the novel also complicates such simplistic claims about human and nonhuman animal behavior. We see that imbrication occur again in *The Dog Stars*. Hig does have a destination in mind, but he only attempts to reach it after the grief of losing Jasper, and the destination is no more rational than is Pi's decision to leave the floating island. "People move because of the wear and tear of anxiety," Pi tells us (79), "in the hope of a better life" (77), and Hig hopes to escape from his sorrow. It is not a threat within his enclosure (the perimeter, his cage) but a threat from within his own being. By not recognizing that agential death is the only way to escape from the ecocollapsed, post-pandemic world and from one's self (as do Frank in *Station Eleven* and the mother in *The Road*), Hig reacts in an illogical way, just as Pi claims that "All living things contain a measure of madness that moves them in strange, sometimes inexplicable ways. This madness can be saving; it is part and parcel of the ability to adapt" (Martel 41). Hig finally safely makes contact with Cima and Pops, and when asked, "Why did you come here?" we are told, "Didn't answer. Not defensive, not reticent, I just didn't know. Not really" (Heller 224). Eventually Hig responds, "My dog died," explaining that he left what is otherwise a safe haven "being at the end of all loss" (224). Indeed, like the roe-deer that quickly returned to their corral and the escaped bear to his enclosure in *Life of Pi*, Hig returns to the comfort of his cage with more to lose by bringing Cima and Pops back with him. The culture of isolation is unsustainable for him while he still finds value in having other people to contribute to his community (an irony I will address shortly).

Consequently, in *The Dog Stars*, staying put within his safe perimeter with food and the militaristic support provided by Bangley seems to enable the best chance of physical survival in many ways, but it is a hopeless survival. Paradoxically, it is when Hig stops following the road in his plane that he finds more to lose, thus giving him a reason to live, as in *The Road*, when the man and boy find the hidden, fully stocked underground bunker when they leave the road. In McCarthy's novel, the road "propels us into our future, rendered to express our worst fears about climate change. [It functions as] the liminal space that carries [the man and boy] endlessly onward."[18] Rather than symbolizing a way to a particular destination, though, McCarthy's road is notable for its absence of purpose. The man and boy intend to end their journey at the ocean, but once they reach it, it is only a minor textual occurrence (230), a disappointment. Following Susan Cutter, Antonia Mehnert defines

---

[18]   Hannah Stark, "'All These Things He Saw and Did Not See': Witnessing the End of the World in Cormac McCarthy's *The Road*," *Critical Survey* 25, no. 2 (2013): 74.

this kind of movement as precipitated on what she calls "global riskscapes," perpetual movement "characterized by the anticipation and experience of a ubiquitous crisis, in which territorial distinctions decline in importance and socio-cultural practices are disembedded from place . . . Since these riskscapes impede any form of re-inhabitation, adaptability and constant renegotiation of the self become key to survival."[19] Within the riskscape, arrival at any specific destination is endlessly deferred: there is no place to inhabit. The man and boy have no future; while the man dies at the end of the novel, the boy is left in the same exact world of violent people and ever-diminishing resources. In *The Dog Stars*, Hig has relative comfort compared to the man and boy, yet he wants to escape from his present reality. He flies to deal with grief and to seek companionship, the voice on the radio, alluding to *The Road* when he says, "I am the keeper of something, not sure what, not the flame, maybe just Jasper" (197) but after Jasper's death, he laments, "Now I don't feel anything. I feel the way my unwadered legs felt after ten minutes in the snow melt. Numb and glad to be. Glad to be numb. The difference maybe between the living and the dead: the living often want to be numb the dead never do, if they never want anything" (158). Hig cannot fully articulate to himself where he is going or why, but flying is a way for him to process and try to carry on with living beyond mere survival. For someone who has a human-vacated world spread around him, the psychology of leaving in search of companionship speaks to the need to create a meaningful humanity in community with others. Hig inhabits a world silent of human sound, instead filled with breaking branches echoing in eardrums no longer accustomed to the steady noise that exists as the background of our own lives, and he seeks human speech rather than food and shelter in an attempt to reconstruct himself by denouncing the status quo. He seeks love, but as I reveal shortly, there is no love to find except in his memories.

The end of *Station Eleven* charts an "awakening world" (Mandel 332), turning away from Kirsten's earlier contemplation of human extinction when she ponders, "If hell is other people, what is a world with almost no people in it? Perhaps soon humanity would simply flicker out, but Kirsten found

---

[19] Antonia Mehnert, *Climate Change Fictions: Representations of Global Warming in American Literature* (Switzerland: Palgrave Macmillan, 2016), 72.

this thought more peaceful than sad. So many species had appeared and later vanished from this earth; what was one more?" (148). Divergently, throughout *The Dog Stars* is horrifying evidence of ecocollapse and species extinction, animals disappearing or migrating and trees dying from beetles and drought. The landscape is covered with dead fields and standing dead trees, "the old seasonal benchmarks mostly nostalgia" in a warmed environment: "We had snow in the mountains this winter but there were two years running where the peaks were dry holding almost nothing. This scared me more than attacks or disease. Losing the trout was bad. Losing the creek is another thing altogether" (Heller 56). The ecocollapse worsens as the post-pandemic years progress with earlier seasonal changes, which Hig marks on a calendar, and we learn that Pop and Cima must leave their hidden ranch because the water source is unreliable. Hig is incredulous that Pops and Cima want to leave their canyon ranch, their "little Eden," but Pops replies, "Last summer the creek almost dried up. We had to dig in the streambed to pool enough water just to drink. Half our cattle died. Pretty much been getting worse every year. Getting warmer, just like they said. . . . If it's drying up here, what is happening off the mesa?" (220). The ranch is the thing Pops loves, what constructs his sense of embedded belonging and identity: "It occurred to me that the death of his grazing land hurt him more, incomparably more than the death of the human race" (221). In an effort to find more water, Pops had tried to dig a well but hit ledge rock so shallow they "can't dig a decent grave" (221). Likewise, Hig does not romanticize: "There is no hyperbole anymore just stark extinction mounting up" (231). The only survival is adaptation that delays the inevitable, so Hig is present. He keeps track. He bears witness.

The state of the ecocollapsed world, then, if not exactly celebrated, is at least honored with a newfound appreciation for beauty wherever it can be found. Psychologists call this post-traumatic growth, defined as "positive psychological change experienced as a result of the struggle with highly challenging life circumstances [that undermine] individuals' ways of understanding the world and their place in it," and includes a radically changed sense of priorities that pay greater attention to "even the smallest joys in life."[20] Whether flying, gardening,

---

[20]   Richard G. Tedeschi and Lawrence G. Calhoun, "Posttraumatic Growth: Conceptual Foundations and Empirical Evidence," *Psychological Inquiry* 15, no. 1 (2004): 1, 6.

fishing, or gazing at the night sky, Hig finds a way to savor time as it unfolds in the present, and even when he remembers the past and all his many losses, he thinks of finding beauty in the simple pleasures of his favorite activities. As Lynn Lozier observes, "Hig's experience is imbued with deep wonder and with tenderness for nature's losses. In this, and in his tentative connections with other people, he struggles with daring to hope while feeling acutely the cost of love and survival."[21] Hig finds beauty in flying (above the earth he cannot see all the ruin) and in fishing, what Bangley scornfully calls "Recreating" (56). In an environment where the fight for survival seems to be all that matters, Hig chooses to absorb himself in outlets where he can experience a deep awareness of beauty. It is transcendence: "This ritual put me in touch with something that felt very pure. Meaning that in fishing I had always all my life brought the best of myself. My attention and carefulness, my willingness to risk, and my love. Patience. Whatever else was going on" (58). Human nature may be red in tooth and claw, but individual humans can make a choice to experience extinction while appreciating the beauty of existence. Hig *loves*, sending his vulnerability out into the diminished world.

Superficially, Hig's emotional potency reiterates the contrast with Bangley, who seems invulnerable because he just kills, without remorse. His character raises the complex issue of what is good or bad when it comes to survival: is it okay to take a life? Is it okay to take property? When? Under what circumstances? In *The Dog Stars*, the truth that everyone has some aspects of "Not Nice" is explicit even when superficially contrasted with people whose actions are so barbaric that they whittle down and define the "fucked up world" made by many of the surviving humans, as further caution against Hig's desire for companionship and his risky need for someone to love him back. For example, Hig finds an abandoned Coke truck full of soda, from which he brings a few cases at a time for him and Bangley to enjoy, providing them piecemeal so as to feel "like a god" (86) alongside Bangley's omniscience. On one trip Hig discovers a group of men hiding inside the truck. "STEP OUT, hands where I can see them," Hig shouts, armed with a loaded automatic rifle. The men comply, and Hig describes them:

---

[21] Lynn Lozier, "Flying over the Future," review of *The Dog Stars*, by Peter Heller, *Science Chronicles Mid-Year Books Issue*, June 2013.

Big hands. Hair on the back dirty. Stuck through the gap they look like a thug trying to do a hand puppet show. Forearms in a blue ski jacket too short for his arms, greasy but new. Door pushed wider. Mallet head, wide blonde dreds, camo bush hat. Tangled beard. A huge man stepping down off the bumper, unwilling to turn his back. (84)

Here, Hig acts to preserve what he feels is his property—but is it, really, in its abandoned state? When he shoots one man who raises a bow from inside the trailer, his objection is "Ruined it. Probably twenty cases of pop" (85), not that he murdered someone to secure a trailer full of Coke. Does he recognize that the soda, from their perspective, is theirs? That they are protecting their own enjoyment of sweet carbonated liquid in the depopulated, ecocollapsed world? Hig is capable of doing so: he imagines their shock watching Jasper eat their dead companion's body after assuring them he will not kill them: "Creates a vortex, a crosscurrent like the two flags at the airport facing each other in contrary winds" (87). Hig commands them to load his plane and plans to leave them with the rest, "sick of defending whatever it is I'm supposed to defend" (87), but then he encounters "Not Nice" and what he sees changes everything: "Pony Tail swung a long necklace of shriveled leather pieces when he bent over. Both of them smelled like death" (88). After a conversation about how Hig is dead anyway because "The A-rabs" have been heard on the radio, Hig asks what the necklace is made of. "[Pony Tail] stood straight, swallowed. His eyes gold green in the last full sun. Mocking. Them are cunts. Dried cunts" (89). Hig pulls the trigger.

Taken on its own, the necklace is gruesome and repugnant, implying that Pony Tail has raped and murdered countless women and then carved off their labia as some sick souvenir (and perhaps not in that order). On the surface, the man is sadistic, reminiscent of serial killers and their collections of flesh, but the dried tissue also recalls Jasper's jerky, made of human flesh, the vulvas representing thousands of female characters in speculative fiction who are objectified and violently abused, and even recall Cima, whose genitals are described as wet during sexual intercourse. Yet readers cannot tell if the necklace is a symbol of hatred or a symbol of reverence, a symbol of life-giving femininity or of life-giving food, or just what it appears on the surface: unnecessary barbarity. The reduction of people to a single desiccated body part, dangling around a man's neck. The reduction of an apocalypse survivor to a single, ghastly necklace. Not knowing the man's motivations almost makes the necklace more gruesome and makes Pony Tail the representation of the depraved who have risen at the end of human civilization. But even then, Hig points out that there are no easy distinctions between the Nice and the Not Nice, struggling with what he has done but not in the way we might expect: "Try to do the right thing. Circumstance intervenes. What am I going to do with twenty cases of Coke? Dole them out to Bangley?" (89). Hig's moral issue is not the killing, nor, as Bangley critiques him, of not getting more information about the voices on the radio "because you discover, oh surprise surprise, that the man is a rapist and killer like every other survivor walking around this goddamn country" (94). The excess Coke is the problem: Hig can no longer dole it out slowly, retaining his value to Bangley.

Thus, the "Not Nice," as I have shown in all of these ecocollapse fictions, is not a static moral code but a spectrum of choices and personal justifications: there is no distinctive "good" or "bad" at the end of humanity, any more than there must have been at the beginning or throughout our species' time on this planet, but *The Dog Stars* works hard to undermine this reading. Once Hig takes off with Pops and Cima (and her goats), seeking more gas and the voice he heard on the radio, they nearly land the plane onto a taut line sprung up along a maintained airstrip, following the instructions from the radio, "All formal, all perfect, by the book, just like before before. Said with a straight face. Like a normal business day at the old airport" (282). A mere 30 feet above the ground, Hig realizes: "The beacon, the tower: the wrecks on the field were scorched like the cars. Can't say I thought anything, nothing reasoned, articulated, there wasn't time. It was just the shock of the image: the burned and crumpled planes. . . . These were crashes" (284). He pulls up sharply and "in the same instant the cable came up. Sprung taut, probably missed my wheels by ten feet. Sprung like a trap. Which is what it was" (285). They decide to land and "get em": "the gut punch feeling of betrayal. All those years, thinking about that radio call. The hope it had engendered. It drove me wild," Hig confesses (285). Pops and Hig attack the tower and kill the elderly man and woman they find inside, justifying their actions because "those cocksuckers invited you out here under false pretenses. Did you see all those goddamn wrecks? How many planes you think they did like that?" (288), like they are the sheriffs of the new world.

Of interest to Hig, Pops, and readers is the ambiguity of what the old man, Samuel, and the old woman, who looks like "Aunt Bee" (292), were doing with any wrecked survivors. Were they eating them? There is no mention of food sources in the description of what Hig and Pops find in their living spaces, although there is discussion of the possibility that they scavenged food and supplies from the wrecked planes. However, it is unlikely that they could have salvaged enough food from burned planes to survive over nine years, and the close presence of three bison indicates they were not likely hunted for food. As Pops asks, "Okay so what did they do with the pissed off survivors?" (288) and the many cats are the biggest clue: "One of the bolder cats was already lapping at the crimson creek" of blood flowing from the dying Samuel (292) even as the event is still unfolding. A reasonable conclusion is that the elderly couple caught human prey to eat them and feed the blood and offal to their cats, who might also be an emergency food supply (they are certainly not pets given that they are confined to one room, which stinks of urine, "the smell. A barrier" [291], and no cats are present in the couple's living space). The elderly couple's macabre collection indicates that hundreds of people have fallen for their trap, too:

> In the room that would have been the living room where the TV might have been, one wall was pegged and on a hundred pegs were caps, mostly baseball caps with the logos of FBOs, aircraft service centers, aviation specialists of all types—cylinders, props, skins—from every corner of the country. The rest of the walls were covered with shelves. On the shelves, alternating, were pairs of spectacles—sunglasses, reading glasses, bifocals, everything. (295)

These material remnants are the couple's collected souvenirs of once-human meat, drawn to their deadly jump cable by a call on the radio.

Such a scenario seems at first glance to be explicitly evil, yet it directly correlates with the setup at Hig's and Bangley's airport at Erie. There, intruders "came singly or in groups, they came with weapons, with hunting rifles, with knives, they came to the porch light I left on like moths to a flame" (9) where they are immediately shot from the berm, no negotiation. Hig leaves the light on in front of an empty house he carefully selected so they can direct any approaching people into their line of fire. Is the porch light equivalent to a radio call? Are the shots fired without warning any different from a taut line across a landing strip? Jasper eats human flesh warm and freshly killed, Hig simply dragging the bodies out of his own sight to retain his sense of righteousness. Hig morally justifies his own use of human flesh for food, too:

> This is what I do, have done: I strip off haunches arms breast buttocks calves. Slice it thin soak in salt brine and dry to jerky for Jasper for the days between. You remember the story of the rugby team in the Andes. The corpses were corpses already dead. They did it to survive. I am no different. I do it for him. I eat venison, bottom fish, rabbit, shiners. I keep his jerky in airtight buckets. He likes it best of all his food I'm sure because of the salt. . . . That we have come to this: remaking our own taboos forgetting the original reasons but still awash in the warnings. (47–8)

The salt indeed. It is unclear if or how Hig keeps their dried meat supplies distinct, loading Jasper's jerky and his own into gallon plastic bags into a backpack "long since over the nausea" (63), calling them both "venison" (114). Can they be distinguished, human jerky from deer jerky? It does not matter. Days after Jasper's death, Hig acknowledges that all meat is the same: "I had eaten all the jerked venison. A hunger deep, ravenous, alive. Had I not thrown out the other meat, Jasper's, I would have eaten it now. Who to judge? What matters if it is he or I, we are the same. But I had emptied the bags on the trail days ago" (117). The only moral restriction is one of external validation—who might judge—in a world where there are very few people left to do so.[22]

In at least one instance, Hig collects living people—he tries to build a community of survivors to work together—and others' collections (the dried vulvas, the caps and glasses, Bangley's guns, Cima's lambs) in contrast could reinstate the sense that there is a definitive moral code of goodness and badness in this ecocollapsed post-pandemic world. Hig's various efforts to preserve a pre-destruction idea of companionship, of semi-normalcy, could be construed as "good" in this structure. Yet the specter of what that community might mean, when its safety demands killing anyone and everyone else,

---

[22] Hig's faith in external validation is reiterated when he is first captured by Cima and Pops. Because Hig himself is the judge when they provide him with lunch, including butter and unlimited milk, he accuses them of cannibalism: "I widened my eyes. You all aren't trying to fatten me up? I mean you've got that taste for human flesh like a rogue shark?" (210).

underlies even that interpretation. *Station Eleven*'s various narrative voices likewise flit between the interwoven conflicts of hope for human community and the dangers of such in recursively contrasting oppositions: "Hell is ~~other people~~ flutes" (Mandel 48) and "Hell is the absence of the people you long for" (144) about those same members of the Travelling Symphony. Similarly, "They were afraid of everyone who wasn't them" (176) and "If you are the light, if your enemies are darkness, then there's nothing that you cannot justify. There's nothing you can't survive, because there's nothing that you will not do" (139). Jeevan is both "a small, insignificant thing, drifting down the shore" and flourishingly "never felt so alive" (193). Pieter Vermeulen observes that "by articulating the threat of biological extinction with accounts of different communities situated before, during, and after the epidemic [*Station Eleven* entangles] its accounts of individual and shared lives . . . just as it juxtaposes its sense of inevitable doom with a resolute hope in the persistence of human culture."[23] In contrast, Hig's flight to find other people, told only through his recollections and remembered conversations, exposes a suicidal ideology rather than one that believes in a regrowth of something resembling human culture.

Some have argued that *The Dog Stars* has a happy ending that imagines the regeneration of community and humanity because Hig finds a partner in Cima, and Pops and Bangley can play checkers and discuss weapons and defensive strategies. For instance, Alan Cheuse claims that "an elegy for a lost world turns suddenly into a paean to new possibilities," what he calls "a new and rejuvenating way of life."[24] Heather Duncan and Eleanor Gold read *The Dog Stars* as revealing "the promise of a brighter future for the few remaining survivors."[25] Lynn Lozier says, "It's a moving, bizarrely hopeful song."[26] Indeed, it is tempting to see the beginnings of a new society forming. Humans are physically weak social creatures, which creates a deep need to band together

[23]   Vermeulen, "Beauty That Must Die," 12.
[24]   Alan Cheuse, "'The Dog Stars' by Peter Heller," review of *The Dog Stars*, by Peter Heller, *The Boston Globe*, August 15, 2012.
[25]   Heather Duncan and Eleanor Gold, "Abject Permanence: Apocalyptic Narratives and the Horror of Persistence," in *Green Matters: Ecocultural Functions of Literature*, ed. Maria Loschnigg and Melanie Braunecker (Leiden, The Netherlands: Brill, 2019), 205. Duncan and Gold only mention Heller's novel in passing, as in contrast to Jeff VanderMeer's *Southern Reach Trilogy*, the focus of their chapter.
[26]   Lozier, "Flying," 7.

for safety and comradeship. Cima and Pops also add practical skills in animal husbandry and horticulture to the Erie partnership structure. Their friendships are an end to loneliness, and as I suggested above, relationships are vital toward moving their group beyond mere survival and into a recognizable state of human culture and flourishing. Companionship thus superficially challenges the post-apocalyptic reality: all surviving humans have disintegrated into little pockets of existence and resistance to each other; the bigger the pocket of existence, the greater the parallel that existence can be to some version of the Before. Yet such a reading fails to attend to elements of the novel that cast doubt on such an alluring determination, including its many allusions to Lionel and his canine companion in Mary Shelly's *The Last Man* (1826), thought to be the first post-pandemic climate fiction novel. Everything humans are using to survive has an expiration date: fuel goes stale; mechanics fail; supplies become tainted or consumed. Furthermore, an attentive analysis reveals that their little group cannot regenerate the human species. Hig: "an old man at forty" (35). Bangley: attacked by marauders, suffered arteriosclerosis. Cima: chronically ill, life expectancy mid-fifties. Pops: aged. Jasper: dead. Melissa: dead. Mennonites: diseased, dying. The Arabs: "never answered my calls" (319). Hig's world has no reproductive futurity.

Rather than an optimistic ending to the novel that leaves readers with hope for a regenerating human species, I find instead that Hig is reminiscing, looking back as the last witness, reporting and recording human extinction like the unnamed narrator in Helen Simpson's "Diary of an Interesting Year" who assumes no reader but writes anyway. *The Dog Stars* is written in the past tense except when interrupted by occasional passages marked off with asterisks in present progressive: the verbs of memory and recollection. Events are blurred and enfolded within the narrative structure, and careful scrutiny of the text reveals that Hig is the last human survivor at Erie (and clues to that fact have been present from the very beginning). The novel opens with an introduction, "My name is Hig, one name. Big Hig if you need another" (3), as though what follows is a journal written to someone not present. Hig discloses, "There is no one to tell this to and yet it seems very important to get this right. The reality and what it is like to escape it. That even now it is sometimes too beautiful to bear" (50), his escapes of reality found in flying, fishing, finding beauty in the land. Celebrating his fortieth birthday, Hig invites Melissa nine years after her death, "and she came the way she does, a whisper and a shiver" (10), never completely erased from his life experience. An asterisked interruption toward the end reveals that the environment might be adapting and rejuvenating, but there is no human present in the passage except Hig's "I": "The buffalo are moving down to their old range, the wolves, the bighorn too. The trout are gone, the elk, but. I've seen osprey up on Jasper's creek, and bald eagles. Plenty of mice in the world, plenty of hawks. Plenty of crows. In winter the trees are full of them. Who needs Christmas decorations?" (295). To unpack the elements of this passage is to realize that even though it intrudes on Hig's past-tense recollection of safely leaving the Grand Junction airport with Pops and Cima, its change in verb tense and use of the singular "I" expose his status as the last survivor, interjecting his present into the narrative storytelling about his past experiences.

Readers know not to trust Hig's mental or psychological narrative reliability, so it is also worth considering why we might want the novel to end on an optimistic note. Specifically, Hig tells us to "be the judge" of the soundness of his mind after "two straight weeks of fever, three days 104 to 105, I know it cooked my brains. Encephalitis or something else. Hot. Thoughts that once belonged, that felt at home with each other, were now discomfited, unsure, depressed" (8). Hig states directly that the relayed experiences narrated in the novel are memories or maybe even just dreams: "I don't know the difference anymore between dream and memory. I wake from dream into dream and am not sure why I keep going. That I suspect only curiosity keeps me alive. That I'm not sure any longer if that is enough" (245). If there were still other people around to give him a sense of community and purpose, "curiosity" would not be the only thing motivating Hig toward the future. Like the unnamed narrator in "Diary," he writes, recording for an unimaginable, implausible posterity using perhaps the last residue of what makes us human: hope. He can only be the last survivor.

Further evidence in support of this interpretation resides in the final lines of the novel, a recitation of Hig's favorite poem by the late Tang poet Li Shangyin (813–858 CE) relayed as "When Will I Be Home?" The poem:

When will I be home? I don't know.

In the mountains, in the rainy night,

The Autumn lake is flooded.

Someday we will be back together again.

We will sit in the candlelight by the West window.

And I will tell you how I remembered you

Tonight on the stormy mountain. (320)[27]

Despite tempting interpretations that make Li Shangyin's living wife the recipient of this poem because of "its prospective scene of domestic intimacy, in which the couple's current separation will become something to talk about when they are together,"[28] biographers have shown that Li Shangyin's wife had died before his term of service in Ba. Rather than a poem literally sent to his wife, then, the poem reflects what Ge Fei identifies as "a blurring of the boundaries between the real and the imagined and with the conflation of different dimensions of time."[29] Michelle Yeh describes Li Shangyin's "evocation of the past" as a complication of traditional Chinese poetic symbolism:

> If, imagistically, the [mountain's] height provides the poet with a panoramic view of space, symbolically the sweeping view engages him in a reflection on time that encompasses an equally expansive scope of the past, present, and future. The nature of such solitary contemplation . . . is more often melancholy than cheerful, more likely elegiac that celebrating, because the present is inevitably seen as a decline from past splendor and the permanence of nature as a poignant reminder of human transience.[30]

The poem included in *The Dog Stars* further extends the reminder of *human* transience into *environmental* transience, which floods from the autumn

[27] This translation of the poem is found in Kenneth Rexroth's *One Hundred More Poems from the Chinese: Love and the Turning Year* (New York: New Directions Publishing, 1970), 77. However, in Stephen Owen's translation, it is alternatively titled as "Night Rain: Sent North" and translated as "You ask the date for my return; / no date is set yet; / night rain in the hills of Ba / floods the autumn pools. / When will we together trim / the candle by the western window / and discuss these times of the night rain / in the hills of Ba?" By choosing the Rexroth rather than the Owen translation, Heller removes the speaker's addressee as an agent from the poem. See Stephan Owen, *The Late Tang: Chinese Poetry of the Mid-Ninth Century (827–860)* (Cambridge, MA: Harvard University Press, 2006), 351.
[28] Owen, *The Late Tang*, 351.
[29] Paola Iovene, *Tales of Futures Past: Anticipation and the Ends of Literature in Contemporary China* (Stanford: Stanford University Press, 2014), 109.
[30] Michelle Yeh, *Modern Chinese Poetry: Theory and Practice Since 1917* (New Haven, CT: Yale University Press, 1991), 8.

rains, Hig's flights likewise providing him a panoramic view of the earth with which to reflect on the past.

We know Hig never had the chance to share his favorite poem with Cima during one of their long nighttime conversations,[31] so why does the poem itself, in italics, stand as his last epistolary message to readers? The poem's last four lines are especially telling: if Cima were alive, Hig would not reminisce about the days they were together, sitting together under the trees at the canyon ranch or within the boundaries of their compound. He would not have to "remember" her because she would still be present. Longing and loss are intertwined, both in the poem and in Hig's experience. By closing the novel in this way, Heller suggests its entirety is the report of a lonely man desperately trying to memorialize his experience, a tale told to no one but the readers of today because there is no "you" at "home" to otherwise tell the story. Thus, in contrast to the ambiguous ending of *The Road*'s final paragraph, *The Dog Stars* makes explicit that Hig is all alone, the last survivor of human species extinction, retaining the last grasp of connection to deceased other people by therapeutically writing to recollect the past, recording the final destruction of human exceptionalism, and bearing witness to human-inclusive extinction.

By representing a post-pandemic depopulated landscape intertwined with global warming, *The Dog Stars* reveals the end events of the collapse of civilization and biological mass extinction while largely dodging the massive social unrest seen in other climate change fictions, which allows us to imagine other species might have a better chance to adapt and flourish if humans were suddenly taken out of the global carbon equation. Humans have gone extinct alongside the trout, elk, and some tree species, but life itself will persevere in a final blow to human exceptionalism: "A lot of songbirds vanished even before, but in this world the raptors seem to be doing fine. A hawk's world," Hig says (150). Like the allusion to the survival of some unseen "life in the deep" in McCarthy's novel, Heller's *The Dog Stars* reminds us that earth's other creatures might adapt and regenerate new types of flourishing in the ecocollapsed world, which we will explore further in Chapter 5.

---

[31]   " 'Hey, I murmured, wanna hear my favorite poem? It was written in the ninth century, in China.'
I thought she was thinking medical thoughts, but then I felt her twitch against me. Not the nightmare twitches Jasper sometimes had but the twitch of falling, of letting go" (317).

5

Loose Ends

The radically estranged, ecocollapsed fictional worlds examined in this book demonstrate embodied natureculture entanglements wherein human life-and-death processes become complex forms of bodily materiality, agency, and precarity within the cannibalistic cultures of human extinction. The existential threats these characters confront might lead some readers to conclude that their desperation excuses any immoral behavior toward other beings, but as my analysis has shown, it is only through the lens of human exceptionalism that the idea of "morality" exists in the first place. "If we appreciate the foolishness of human exceptionalism," Donna Haraway insists, "then we know that becoming is always becoming *with*—in a contact zone where the outcome, where who is in the world, is at stake."[1] For not being morally instructive speculations with clearly identified human heroes and villains, these ecocollapse fictions enable interpretive moves that are unsparing in their dismantling of human superiority, demonstrating how individuals exist as parts of active landscapes of coevolutionary processes, human and nonhuman, political, cultural, environmental, racialized, gendered, and objectified in constant, contextualized interchanges. Hubert Zapf calls this kind of mutuality "reintegrative interdiscourse" that demonstrates ways "the dichotomies of mind and body, intellect and emotion, culture and nature are overcome . . . in ecosemiotic networks of signs."[2] Humans are as much embroiled in climate change as any other

---

[1] Donna Haraway, *When Species Meet* (Minneapolis: University of Minnesota Press, 2007), 244.
[2] Hubert Zaph, "Literary Ecology and the Ethics of Texts," *New Literary History* 38, no. 4 (2008): 13. See also Zaph, "Creative Matter and Creative Mind: Cultural Ecology and Literary Creativity" in *Material Ecocriticism*, ed. Serenella Iovino and Serpil Oppermann (Bloomington: University of Indiana Press, 2014), 51–66.

living thing, and by facing the extinction of the human species in these fictions, readers are forced to confront their own anthropocentric biases and "explore the emotional complexity of our responses to the threat [of extinction]," as Richard Kerridge suggests.[3] Troublingly, according to Jamil Zaki, "When people experience anxiety in response [to mortality], they seek out whatever makes them feel safe, including the comfort of their own tribe . . . and become more hostile toward outsiders."[4] By deferring the last death, the narrative forms of these fictions ease readers gently toward the notion of species extinction.[5]

We cannot witness the actual last death, that of the writer/narrator in the epistolary "Diary of an Interesting Year" and *The Dog Stars*, or of the inscrutable boy in *The Road*. The texts simply *end*, by virtue of the narrative requirements, which invites readers and leaves open further considerations. This brief delay allows readers their own personal experiences of "what things feel like," as Bill McKibben says,[6] prompting thoughts about personal legacies that Zaki argues "encourage people to sacrifice for future generations, for example, by engaging in sustainable activities to address climate change" (196) and otherwise "build kindness toward future generations" (248).[7] Similarly in Serenella Iovino's judgment, the opportunity of what she calls "narrative reinhabitation" becomes a vehicle for ethical consideration: "From an ethical standpoint, the [imagined] epilogue of a story is a task rather than an accomplished reality. By telling a story, narrations not only confer a shape (namely, a sense) to the events that happen in a given context, making them understandable; they

[3]   Richard Kerridge, "The Single Source," *Ecozon@* 1, no. 1 (2010): 159. doi: 10.37536/ECOZONA.2010.1.1.334.
[4]   Jamil Zaki, *The War for Kindness: Building Empathy in a Fractured World* (New York: Crown Publishing Group, 2019), 172–3. Subsequent citations appear parenthetically in the text.
[5]   As I discuss in Chapter 1, Dipesh Chakrabarty rightly interrogates the notion of a human "species" before calling for a "new universal history" that Nicholas Mirzoeff further problematizes in "It's Not the Anthropocene, It's the White Supremacy Scene; or, The Geological Color Line." I think we can experience ourselves as individuals and extrapolate to wider and wider circles of concern and thus experience extinction conceptually, while agreeing with Mirzoeff that the boundary marker of "the Anthropocene" pays inadequate attention to imperialism and colonial genocide.
[6]   Bill McKibben, introduction to *I'm with the Bears: Short Stories from a Damaged Planet*, ed. Mark Martin (London: Verso, 2011), 3.
[7]   Zaki cites Liza Zaval et al., "How Will I Be Remembered? Conserving the Environment for the Sake of One's Legacy," *Psychological Science* 26, no. 2 (2015): 231–6 and Kimberly A. Wade-Benzoni et al., "It's Only a Matter of Time: Death, Legacies, and Intergenerational Decisions," *Psychological Science* 23, no. 7 (2012): 704–9.

also creatively enable a project that takes on society and its values."[8] Readers of these novels are thus encouraged to participate in the fluid potentiality of the last witness's future experience.[9] We can visualize it, in fact, as part of our human ability to fantasize, perhaps optimistically imagining a peaceful death for the last human, like David Quammen envisions the death of the last dodo:

> In the dark of an early morning in 1667, say, during a rainstorm, she took cover beneath a cold stone ledge at the base of one of the Black River cliffs. She drew her head down against her body, fluffed her feathers for warmth, squinted in patient misery. She waited. She didn't know it, nor did anyone else, but she was the only dodo on Earth. When the storm passed, she never opened her eyes. This is extinction.[10]

Hig in *The Dog Stars* contemplates a similar end: "I was wondering: Is this what it's like to die? To be this alone? To hold to a store of love and pass over?"[11] Readers also have available to their futuristic imaginings the emotional resonance from images of the starvation shudders of a polar bear cub, horrific violence and death in the daily news, the ravaged bodies of people dying of disease, or any number of other conditions to visualize the last witness's final end. There are innumerable ways to die in the Anthropocene.

But following Timothy Clark's call in *Ecocriticism on the Edge* that "environmental readings of literature and culture may need to engage more directly with [their own] delusions of self-importance"[12] in an attempt to "fail better," as Greg Garrard puts it in his promotional endorsement in support of Clark's imperative book, I hesitate to make any claims about larger social or cultural or political *systemic* outcomes from my analysis of human extinction in these works. Doing so is tempting: this book could then follow the successful narrative structure found in the thousands of fictional plotlines that

---

8   Serenella Iovino, "Restoring the Imagination of Place: Narrative Reinhabitation and the Po Valley," in *The Bioregional Imagination: Literature, Ecology, and Place*, ed. Tom Lynch, Cheryll Glotfelty, and Karla Armbruster (Athens: University of Georgia Press, 2010), 106.

9   According to Mikhail Bakhtin in *The Dialogic Imagination*, "open-endedness" is one of the defining features of the novel as a genre.

10 David Quammen, *The Song of the Dodo: Island Biogeography in an Age of Extinctions* (New York: Scribner, 1996), 275.

11 Peter Heller, *The Dog Stars* (New York: Vintage, 2013), 161. Subsequent citations appear parenthetically in the text.

12 Timothy Clark, *Ecocriticism on the Edge: The Anthropocene as a Threshold Concept* (London: Bloomsbury Academic, 2015), 198. Subsequent citations appear parenthetically in the text.

make for compelling stories in part by ending with a happy outcome (novels of the sort I discarded for that very reason at the outset of this study). Many examinations of climate change or post-apocalyptic fiction conclude with messages of transformative optimism[13] because, as Clark elucidates, "The hope in environmental criticism has been that cultural change can form a kind of inverse of the tragedy of the commons, a self-multiplying social and psychic force strong enough to prevail" against a multitude of forces that prevent or limit immediate, effective, global responses to climate change (197). Even books in the emerging human extinction genre of creative nonfiction writing[14] tend to conclude with advice about personal adaptations that might somehow create the social change necessary to minimize the cascade effects of runaway global warming or otherwise encourage confidence, including Peter Brannen's *The Ends of the World* (2017), Fred Guterl's *The Fate of the Species* (2013), Clive Hamilton's *Requiem for a Species* (2010), Elizabeth Kolbert's *Field Notes from a Catastrophe* (2006), Nicholas P. Money's *The Selfish Ape: Human Nature and Our Path to Extinction* (2019),[15] Naomi Oreskes and Eric M. Conway's *The Collapse of Western Civilization: A View from the Future* (2014), Roy Scranton's *Learning to Die in the Anthropocene* (2015), and Alan Weisman's *A World Without Us* (2007). Works that are explicitly about doomsday survival strategies—build your own bunker!—are legion, and they reinforce tribal concretization in unhelpful ways. Works focusing on methods for retaining psychological health amid climate change are less common but include Sarah Jaquette Ray's *A Field Guide to Climate Anxiety* (2020); Carolyn Baker's *Love*

---

[13] For example, Antonia Mehnert's *Climate Change Fictions: Representations of Global Warming in American Literature* (Switzerland: Palgrave Macmillan, 2016) explicitly focuses only on those examples "that leave room for hope" (124), arguing that apocalyptic endings do not have the persuasive power to prompt readers to take action against climate change. Andrew Tate's *Apocalyptic Fiction* ends with a tentative optimism following his analysis of Mandel's *Station Eleven*. See also Timothy Clark's many examples of ecocritics' "overinvestments in the power of cultural representations [and] the social importance of art and literature" (196) in *Ecocriticism on the Edge*.

[14] These books are rooted in journalism, science, sociology, psychology, anthropology, paleontology, politics, and other disciplines, but the more-speculative examples do not fit in either fiction or nonfiction genre categories, being a kind of creative non/fiction. Perhaps they should be called "futuristic nonfiction"? Stephanie LeMenager's essay "Climate Change and the Struggle for Genre" in *Anthropocene Reading* suggests the genre be called cli-fi in "the novelistic mode" (222), emphasizing "mode" to reflect her optimism that the genre can spur effective social action.

[15] Nicholas Money's otherwise cynical reflection about the species he calls *Homo narcissus* particularly surprised me: it concludes with the line, "And who knows, if we are nicer, maybe things will keep running for longer than we expect" (110). Happy endings are so innate to storytelling structures that they seem nearly impossible to resist.

in the Age of Ecological Apocalypse (2015); Robert Bringhurst and Jan Zwicky's *Learning to Die: Wisdom in the Age of Climate Crisis* (2018); much of E. Ann Kaplan's work, including *Climate Trauma* (2016); and Roy Scranton's book listed above. Bill McKibben's *Falter: Has the Human Game Begun to Play Itself Out?* (2019) concludes with a meditation on human solidarity:

> Another name for human solidarity is love, and when I think about our world in its present form, that is what overwhelms me. The human love that works to feed the hungry and clothe the naked, the love that comes together in defense of sea turtles and sea ice and all else around us that is good. The love that lets each of us see we're not the most important thing on earth, and makes us okay with that. The love that welcomes us, imperfect, into the world and surrounds us when we die.[16]

These types of works are—with few exceptions—often presumptuous and conclude hopefully; they attempt to shock readers into action but simultaneously define climate change as a challenge that can be overcome or beaten rather than an entangled, irreversible, and accelerating complexity without an external enemy to fight. They are deeply committed to human exceptionalism that suggests only the distinctly human capacities that created high-carbon societies can also save us from the consequences of global climate change even as untold other species go extinct.

The relentless efforts found in thousands upon thousands of such warnings over many decades have been unsuccessful at creating a transformational force. George Marshall uncovers some of the complex reasons why in his unsettling *Don't Even Think about It: Why Our Brains Are Wired to Ignore Climate Change* (2014).[17] One of the many difficulties he explicates is definitional:

> We can define climate change as an economic problem, a technological problem, a moral problem, a human rights problem, an energy problem, a social justice problem, a land use problem, a governance problem, an ideological battle between left and right worldviews, or a lack of respect for God's creation. Each approach will generate different responses, different ways to share the costs, and especially, different language with which to

16 Bill McKibben, *Falter: Has the Human Game Begun to Play Itself Out?* (New York: Henry Holt, 2019), 256.
17 George Marshall, *Don't Even Think about It: Why Our Brains Are Wired to Ignore Climate Change* (London: Bloomsbury, 2014). Subsequent citations appear parenthetically in the text.

justify action. Or inaction, because some people will refuse to accept that climate change is a problem at all. (96)

Ecocollapse Fiction and Cultures of Human Extinction certainly cannot presume to tip the scale toward systemic transformational change, and as Marshall argues, "A single personal sacrifice [of the kind emphasized in rich Western countries as lifestyle changes encouraging reduced consumption, simplicity, and locality] is meaningless unless it is supported by wider systemic and social change" (200).[18] We simultaneously live in a culture of individualism in a world where nearly everything to change is beyond individual control.

Instead, my expectation is that these speculations of human extinction can provide *empathetic intelligibility* to an issue that is otherwise incomprehensible in the destabilized and destabilizing Anthropocene. Realistic examples of ecocollapse and human extinction have the capacity to help us individually imagine beyond the vague notion of "species extinction" and toward an acceptance of death itself that can raise evocative potential as we imagine diminishing futures and a larger reckoning with collective issues and the uneven distribution of risks. The damaging repercussions of colonialism, global inequality, and climate change have virtually ensured that, as Suketu Mehta attests, "mass migration is *the* defining human phenomenon of the twenty-first century. Never before has there been so much human movement."[19] In *Climate Change Fictions: Representations of Global Warming in American Literature*, Antonia Mehnert shows how representational narratives "serve as a way for readers and viewers to empathize with people across time, and thus with future generations, as well as with people in different social, economic, and ethnic contexts."[20] But as Ulrich Beck observes, "We are all now moral entrepreneurs laden with personal responsibility but with no access to the actual decisions [at the systemic level]."[21] One benefit of my analyses of ecocollapse fictions and

---

[18] This is not to say that those of us living high-carbon lifestyles should not try to reduce our deleterious effects, just that those efforts are not in themselves solutions to the "wicked problem" of climate change; are inevitably contradictory; and can cascade into various never-ending questions of "better than what?" that can lead to anxiety, guilt, and feelings of powerlessness. Alexis Shotwell illustrates the complexity of such ideals of ethical purity in *Against Purity: Living Ethically in Compromised Times* (Minneapolis: University of Minnesota Press, 2016).

[19] Suketu Mehta, *This Land Is Our Land: An Immigrant's Manifesto* (New York: Farrar, Straus and Giroux, 2019), 6.

[20] Mehnert, *Climate Change Fictions*, 88.

[21] Ulrich Beck, *World at Risk*, trans. Ciaran Cronin (Cambridge: Polity, 2009), 169.

their cultures of human extinction is the complication of exceptionalist moral values, challenging traditional definitions of moral considerability in ways that enable recognition of climate change as a problem without a standard "enemy" narrative. As Marshall argues about rhetorical attacks on climate deniers, "The missing truth, deliberately avoided, in these enemy narratives, is that in high-carbon societies, everyone contributes to the emissions that cause the problem and everyone has a strong reason to ignore the problem or to write their own alibi" (42). Thus, rather than concluding this book with resigned fatalism or false hope, I here emphasize what individuals can control, as exhibited through the textual analysis in previous chapters. Following Stephanie LeMenager's claim that "the project of the Anthropocene novel . . . is at best a project of paying close attention to what it means to live through climate shift, moment by moment, in individual, fragile bodies,"[22] this chapter illustrates what Haraway calls "staying with the trouble": "Staying with the trouble requires learning to be truly present, not as a vanishing pivot between awful or Edenic pasts and apocalyptic or salvific futures, but as mortal critters entwined in myriad unfinished configurations of places, times, matters, meanings."[23] The subtlety of these fictions' extinctions and the brief deferment of the last death help frame adaptation to changing environments without structuring a defense for their causes, instead enabling acceptance that these extinction events are happening, will happen, might happen to us individually or to the people we love. Acceptance can lead to peace with the notion of change and the impermanence of all things, which leaves space for compassion, empathy, and action without fear. These responses pertain to the development of what Kate Rigby identifies in *Dancing with Disaster* as "modes of personal and collective comportment that are no longer premised on certitude . . . but that instead presuppose the unforeseeable."[24] As I have shown, the characters examined in previous chapters demonstrate many of these adaptive features, as mortal "critters" no longer deluded by human exceptionalism in ecocollapsed worlds.

---

[22] Stephanie LeMenager, "Climate Change and the Struggle for Genre," in *Anthropocene Reading: Literary History in Geologic Times*, ed. Tobias Menely and Jesse Oak Taylor (University Park: Pennsylvania State University Press, 2017), 225.

[23] Donna Haraway, *Staying with the Trouble: Making Kin in the Chthulucene* (Durham, NC: Duke University Press, 2016), 1.

[24] Kate Rigby, *Dancing with Disaster: Environmental Histories, Narratives, and Ethics for Perilous Times* (Charlottesville: University of Virginia Press, 2015), 20.

Hig's attitude in Peter Heller's *The Dog Stars* is a fruitful place to begin further consideration: he says, "Nothing to lose . . . *You are already dead*" (130), an attitude that enables a productive opportunity to consider the influence of psychological states like acceptance. The fear of death, which Marshall correlates with the refusal to accept the reality of climate change, problematizes acceptance that extinction might really happen because the death denial is foundational to human psychology. As Aminatta Forna puts it in her novel *The Memory of Love*, "It doesn't take courage to survive, it takes cowardice."[25] Judith Butler's philosophical explication in "The Desire to Live" shows why: Spinoza posits self-preservation—the denial of death—as a precondition of virtuous life, whereas for Levinas, "self-preservation cannot be the basis of ethics" because it establishes a "relation to the self as prior to the relation to the other," a "social world in which the individual is primary, and in which ethical obligations fail to be acknowledged."[26] Here we can take a lesson from Yann Martel's *Life of Pi*, wherein ethical obligations and shared precarity are continuously acknowledged in joint humility with Richard Parker. Like Hig, Pi "had lost all fear of death and resolved to die,"[27] acquiescing to its inevitability. Following a multitude of philosophers in various traditions, Roy Scranton emphasizes accepting death in *Learning to Die in the Anthropocene*, arguing that "learning to die demands daily cultivation of detachment and daily reminders of mortality" to overcome the fear of death that precludes "adapting, with mortal humility, to our new reality" in the Anthropocene.[28] In Cormac McCarthy's *The Road*, the father is unable to concede to death, instead forging an attachment to the boy that becomes a "sentimental abstraction" in the sense articulated by Lauren Berlant in *Cruel Optimism*.[29] As she demonstrates, the "history of sentimentality around children that sees

---

[25] Aminatta Forna, *The Memory of Love* (London: Bloomsbury, 2010). Forna's character Adrian alludes to the "fragmentation of conscience" from M. Scott Peck's *People of the Lie*, from which Forna quotes directly in her Acknowledgments.

[26] Judith Butler, "The Desire to Live," in *Senses of the Subject* (New York: Fordham University Press, 2015), 71, 78.

[27] Yann Martel, *Life of Pi: A Novel* (Orlando, FL: Harcourt, Inc. 2001), 241. Subsequent citations appear parenthetically in the text.

[28] Roy Scranton, *Learning to Die in the Anthropocene: Reflections on the End of Civilization* (San Francisco, CA: City Lights Books, 2015), 92, 23. See also Atul Gawande's *Being Mortal: Medicine and What Matters at the End* (New York: Picador, 2014) for how a sense of mortality shifts human perspective and reorders human desires.

[29] Lauren Berlant, *Cruel Optimism* (Durham, NC: Duke University Press, 2011), 35.

them as the reason to have optimism [is tangled with the notion that] their lives are not already ruined," yet the boy lives in a "blighted field" of ruined ecocollapse.[30] The boy is an object to the father, representing his delusional hope for the future. In contrast are the mother in *The Road* and the narrator in Helen Simpson's "Diary of an Interesting Year," who strive to spare their children greater suffering as subjects in ecocollapsed worlds where human exceptionalism finds no purchase. Acceptance of death as part of the ecological cycles of all life reduces human exceptionalism and individuality in a way that promotes intersubjective responsibility rather than objectification.

Pi's intersubjective, empathetic entanglement with the living and nonliving multiplicitous world illustrates the effectiveness of trans-corporeal embeddedness as seen in *Life of Pi*, his "I" cluttered, to use the words of Judith Butler in *Precarious Life*, "with signs of its undoing": "When we are speaking about the 'subject' we are not always speaking about an individual: we are speaking about a model for agency and intelligibility, one that is very often based on notions of sovereign power. At the most intimate levels, we are social; we are comported toward a 'you'; we are outside ourselves, constituted in cultural norms that precede and exceed us, given over to a set of cultural norms and a field of power that condition us fundamentally."[31] Elusive as epistemological decidability may be in the novel, the material world is powerfully agential, and Pi inscribes an ethos of reciprocity and ethical regard for individuals of all kinds as part of a multispecies collective. Pi and Richard Parker might be read alongside the characters in Amitav Ghosh's novel *The Hungry Tide* (2006), who expose the valuing of international tiger conservation efforts in India over the daily lives of people—people so poor that their predation by a tiger is not even reported: "It happens every week that people are killed by tigers. How about the horror of that? If there were killings on that scale anywhere else on Earth, it would be called a genocide, and yet here it goes almost unremarked: these killings are never reported, never written about in the papers. And the reason is just that these people are too poor to matter. We all know it, but we choose not to see it."[32] Ghosh complicates easy binaries of economic, political, and

[30] Ibid., 171.
[31] Judith Butler, *Precarious Life: The Powers of Mourning and Violence* (London: Verso, 2004), 23, 45.
[32] Amitav Ghosh, *The Hungry Tide* (Boston, MA: Houghton Mifflin Harcourt, 2006), 248.

conservationist rhetoric in the figure of Roy, who unsettles their structural logic: "Just suppose," she says, "we crossed that imaginary line that prevents us from deciding that no other species matters except ourselves. What'll be left then? . . . And do you think it'll stop at that? Once we decide we can kill off other species, it'll be people next—just the kind of people you're thinking of, the people who are poor and unnoticed."[33] Pi's rich, ambiguous experience in *Life of Pi* even more effectively deprioritizes the "I" of human exceptionalism and levels Cartesian dualisms into intersubjective, simultaneous connectedness and entanglement in valuable ways.

Life of Pi further illustrates that the structures of colonialism are deeply complicit in many global inequities, helping direct the focus of analysis toward imperative issues of justice and injustice. The novel engages with interwoven consequences of decolonization and its effects on formerly subjugated peoples in India, including various religious, political, and social legacies. Postcolonial political and social instability is the root cause of Pi's lifeboat experience, positioning readers toward the structural links between colonialism, racism, and various asymmetries of power that result in social, political, and economic upheavals.[34] Clues for the careful reader are scattered throughout the novel: Pondicherry was the French colonial capital, which is why "Mamaji has two passports. He's Indian and French" (73). Like most Indians at the time, the Patel family does not own their land and sells their zoo animals to leave for Canada after the promise of a "New India" is thwarted by Indira Gandhi's governmental declaration of Emergency on June 26, 1975 and the subsequent institution of numerous repressive measures—the "troubled times in India" Pi alludes to (78). Pi identifies the growing authoritarianism in mid-1970s India as a consequence of (and backlash against) colonial violence and cultural domination, whereby the expectation of "parliamentary government, democratic elections, freedom of speech, freedom of the press, freedom of association, rule of law and everything else enshrined in India's Constitution" (79), suspended by Gandhi's ordinances, creates further instability amid complex sociocultural differences in decolonialized nations. Although the

---

[33] Ibid., 249.
[34] For a thorough explication of *Life of Pi* as a postcolonial novel, see Graham Huggan and Helen Tiffin's *Postcolonial Ecocriticism: Literature, Animals, Environment* (New York: Routledge, 2010).

fictional Patel family does not own their home or the zoo property, they do own the zoo animals, and selling them enables their departure from India to Canada: they are not members of India's powerless poor, who were confronted with numerous oppressive autocratic ordinances that resulted in forced labor camps, starvation, and death. The "Emergency," described by Ved Mehta in 1977, "will be remembered as an extraordinarily Orwellian passage of time in an ancient land."[35] Grieving the loss of place and identity, the Patel family boards a cargo ship that is itself a metaphor for globalism: registered in Panama, owned by a Japanese company, captained by English-speaking men, crewed by Taiwanese sailors, served by a French cook, named for a Jewish mysticism, and transporting human and nonhuman animals from all over the world: capitalism on a grand scale. Pi's shipwrecked experience disavows and repudiates exploitative practices and inequalities, demanding recognition of the particular justice claims expressed in a single question: "If there's only one nation in the sky, shouldn't all passports be valid for it?" (74). The December 2019 Oxfam International report, "Forced from Home: Climate-Fueled Displacement," proves that the people least responsible for climate change are already being displaced by fires, floods, and cyclones.[36] There is one livable earth, and as the livable places inevitably shrink, climate refugees should be welcomed.

Environmental injustice exacerbates existing structural inequalities in complex ways in these fictions, and questions of power, privilege, and systemic oppression are further written into the reordering of worlds as their horizons contract. Helen Simpson's "Diary of an Interesting Year" incorporates climate asylum seekers, and importantly, the narrator's fear of the refugees is exposed as a source of vulnerability rather than empowerment: she and G are dangerously unskilled at interpreting either the social environment in their apartment or the physical environment they abandon it for. The us/them formulation succinctly characterized in their "stash of tins under the bedroom floorboards"[37] can be identified as a dereliction of the duty of care and empathy toward suffering,

---

[35] Ved Mehta, "The New India of Indira Gandhi," *The New Yorker*, February 14, 1977, 101. Archived online.

[36] Oxfam International, "Forced from Home: Climate-Fueled Displacement," December 2, 2019.

[37] Helen Simpson, "Diary of an Interesting Year" in *In-Flight Entertainment: Stories* (New York: Alfred A. Knopf, 2012), 149. Subsequent citations appear parenthetically in the text.

racialized others, compounded by communication difficulties and different cultural norms. They fail to embody the categorical imperative of hospitality that recognizes the vulnerability of an other. As Jacques Derrida defines unconditional hospitality, it "consists in welcoming whoever arrives before imposing any conditions on him, before knowing and asking anything at all . . . Hospitality consists in doing everything to address the other, to accord to him, even to ask him his name, while keeping this question from becoming a 'condition,' a police inquisition, a blacklist or a simple border control."[38] While the narrator and G assume houseguest rules will apply, as I suggest in Chapter 3, they set conditions in their assumptions. Perhaps the Spanish grandmother thinks an ethics of respect for the elderly is in place when she takes their bedroom, leaving them to sleep on the kitchen table. By hiding their food rather than sharing it, the narrator and G establish hostility toward outsiders that has repercussions. When the grandmother discovers the canned food, there is no established ethos of reciprocity among the multiple corporeal, environmental, and affective experiences of the people residing in the small apartment together. The source of vulnerability is thus not merely G's and the narrator's post-evacuation ignorance but also a result of their treatment of ecocollapse 'others' before they even leave the apartment.

Usefully, the narrator and G are surprised to find themselves part of the marginalized community despite their educated, previously middle-class comfort, making ecocollapse personal for readers in high-carbon societies who might think they are "safe" from the effects of global climate change (readers of the *New Yorker*, where the story was first published, perhaps). This inclusivity helps make visible what is often elided in climate fiction: the greater suffering of marginalized and poor populations. Antonia Mehnert demonstrates that "While some communities are twice ostracized, displaced by multiple climate events, these dramatic circumstances remain unknown to the rest of the population" in her analysis of climate injustice.[39] In "Diary," the Spanish refugees who have been forcibly displaced from their homes and communities are correlated with the narrator and G in contrast to the protected isolation of "the top layer" in a valuable consideration: the very wealthiest are "hanging

---

[38] Jacques Derrida, "The Principle of Hospitality," *Angelaka* 5, no. 3 (2005): 7.
[39] Mehnert, *Climate Change Fictions*, 196.

on inside their plastic bubbles of filtered air while the rest of us shuffle about with goiters and tumors and bits of old sheet tied over our mouths" (146). Walls and armed guards secure the perimeter: "All the farmland round here is surrounded by razor wire and armed guards" (153). The infiltrators are *us*. As Rob Nixon articulates, "Walls concretize a short-term psychology of denial: the delusion that we can survive long-term in a world whose resources are increasingly unshared," excluding the poor and marginalized "through a literal concretizing of out of sight out of mind."[40] In "Diary," the world's most vulnerable inhabitants expand to include the entirety of the human species, regardless of their previous agency and privilege.

While "Diary" brings attention to the toxic inequalities experienced by poor and other marginalized communities, *The Dog Stars* can be read to value justice and the inclusion of corporeal difference, especially in the character of Cima and the Mennonite community, both of which figure disability, chronic illness, and the interlinking of invisible materiality with the corporeal self. Cima's fragile body makes visible the essential inclusion of marginalized people, especially when she fearlessly interacts with the Mennonite community: a "restoration" as defined by Eli Clare.[41] By asserting intimacy, mutuality, and co-becoming, she transforms Hig's understanding of disability, chronic illness, vulnerability, and risk with her engaged recognition and physical touch, not despite but regardless of their living with a deadly contagious disease. Valuably to these analyses, the Mennonites' illness protects them in a profound antagonism of sickness and safety: "The big signs along the fences at the edge of their fields THE BLOOD. The terror that evoked. The truth of it for anyone with a pair of binoculars to see: the wasted figures bent as if into a stiff wind, the exhausted movements, the hollow eyes. Kept them away, all attackers, preserved their lives as it killed them" (Heller 317). This juxtaposition reconfigures disease and bodily vulnerability into an explicit benefit, providing insights into what dis/ability might mean and how it might transform in ecocollapsed futures toward greater inclusivity, a fundamental aspect of any just society.

---

[40] Rob Nixon, *Slow Violence and the Environmentalism of the Poor* (Cambridge, MA: Harvard University Press, 2011), 20.
[41] Eli Clare, "Meditations on Natural Worlds, Disabled Bodies, and a Politics of Cure," in *Material Ecocriticism*, ed. Serenella Iovino and Serpil Oppermann (Bloomington: University of Indiana Press, 2014), 207.

Cima also illustrates how the kind of emotional flexibility shown in Emile Bruneau's work results in more equally distributed empathy toward both in- and out-groups.[42] What I have elsewhere called "emphatic empathy" is the purposeful, intentional practice of resonating with the frequency of other people's suffering from a place of compassionate detachment rather than practicing defensive dehumanization.[43] Empathy of this sort is difficult and complicated. Zaki defines three interwoven types of empathetic process: cognitive empathy (mentalizing to identify what others feel), emotional empathy (sharing their emotions), and empathetic concern (motivation to improve their experiences). Hig's visits to the Mennonite community demonstrate empathetic concern because bringing them a case of Sprite, fixing a pump, or showing them how to make a fish trap "kinda loosens something inside me. That nearly froze up" (19). But Cima's willingness to touch calls attention to the ramifications of physicality beyond the gaze: "The children reached out, clung to her skirt, one little girl, I think her name was Lily, Lily held her leg like a bear cub hugs a tree. . . . The wonder of being touched by a stranger. No longer untouchable" (315). Cima illustrates how emphatic empathy opens opportunities for "kindred welcoming" (314) in various bodily material interactions within dynamic cultural and physical environments.

In McCarthy's *The Road*, the boy's emphatic empathy toward Ely—despite his father's ongoing objectification of human others—demonstrates what Johanna R. Vollhardt calls "altruism born of suffering"[44] and the value of prosociality and relationship-building even in terrifying situations. According to Zaki, "There is ample evidence to support the claim that intense suffering can lead to increased empathy and prosociality. But in other cases, the opposite is true—violence begets violence, and suffering can make people crueler or

[42]   See Emile G. Bruneau et al., "Parochial Empathy Predicts Reduced Altruism and the Endorsement of Passive Harm," *Social Psychological and Personality Science* 8, no. 8 (2017): 934–42, cited in Zaki.

[43]   See Sarah E. McFarland, "Animal Studies, Literary Animals, and Yann Martel's *Life of Pi*," in *The Cambridge Companion to Literature and the Environment*, ed. Louise Westling (New York: Cambridge University Press, 2014) and "Such Beastly Behavior: Predation, Revenge, and the Question of Ethics," in *Exploring Animal Encounters: Philosophical, Cultural, and Historical Perspectives*, ed. Dominik Ohrem and Matthew Calarco (London: Palgrave Macmillan, 2018).

[44]   Johanna R. Vollhardt, "Altruism Born of Suffering and Prosocial Behavior Following Adverse Life Events: A Review and Conceptualization," *Social Justice Research* 22, no. 1 (2009): 53–97. See also David M. Greenberg et al., "Elevated Empathy in Adults Following Childhood Trauma," *PLoS One* 13, no. 10 (2018), cited in Zaki.

abusive" (188). Zaki posits that mindset malleability (how much or how little people believe they can change their own psychology and behavior) affects whether people might tend toward aggression or empathy in response to particular situations.[45] In contrast is Deborah Bird Rose's proposition to enact participatory, relational ethical responses; she says, "I believe that the current extinction crisis is an Earth-shattering disaster, one that cannot be unmade, and in that sense cannot be mended, but yet one toward which we owe an ethical response that includes turning toward others in the hopes of mending at least some of the damage."[46] The Western literary and cultural heritage that inscribes human exceptionalism and individualism is responsible for denying or eliding ethical standing for various others, but the boy's prosociality in the face of strangers validates the argument that fearless, emphatic empathy, regardless of the consequences to the individual self, is a tenable comportment in catastrophic times, especially once an acceptance of death is achieved.

Remembrance is also key in these fictions, of the kind Roy Scranton calls for: "We must inculcate ruminative frequencies in the human animal by teaching slowness, attention to detail, argumentative rigor, careful reading, and meditative reflection. We must keep up our communion with the dead, for they are us, as we are the dead of future generations."[47] In *The Dog Stars*, Hig models an accordance with environmental and social changes instead of a mastery of climate-changed "nature" and focuses on recording his memories and moments of joy and overwhelming beauty. Like Hig, Pi actively seeks beauty ("The more you look the more you see" [13]) because "At moments of wonder, it is easy to avoid small thinking, to entertain thoughts that span the universe, that capture both thunder and tinkle, thick and thin, the near and the far" (233). Pi too kept a diary: "It's hard to read. I wrote as small as I could. I was afraid I would run out of paper. There's not much to it. Words scratched on a page trying to capture a reality that overwhelmed me" (208). Both Hig and the unnamed narrator of "Diary of an Interesting Year" utilize expressive writing, which has been shown to improve mental health and alleviate depression and anxiety in therapeutic studies. Hig illustrates, "I wonder what it is this need

---

[45]   See Jamil Zaki, "Chapter 1: The Surprising Mobility of Human Nature," in *The War for Kindness: Building Empathy in a Fractured World* (New York: Crown Publishing Group, 2019).

[46]   Deborah Bird Rose, *Wild Dog Dreaming* (Charlottesville: University of Virginia Press, 2011), 5.

[47]   Scranton, *Learning to Die in the Anthropocene*, 108.

to tell. To animate somehow the deathly stillness of the profoundest beauty. Breathe life in the telling" (Heller 52). In these examples, readers encounter the kind of "restorying" of landscapes suggested by David Abram as part of efforts toward "binding the imagination of our bodies back into the wider life of the animate earth."[48] In contrast, in *The Road*, when the boy wants to "write a letter to the good guys. So if they came along they'd know we were here. We could write it up there where it wouldnt get washed away," his father reinscribes fear and risk: "What if the bad guys saw it?"[49] The boy's attempt to record his existence is discouraged rather than empowered, leaving no evidence of his perspective about the ecocollapsed world.

Ecocollapse fictions that forecast human extinction also enable us to account for the ways that extinction plays a significant role in the potential flourishing of other life-forms: this is, after all, the *sixth* great extinction. What might evolve into the new ecosystems of climate-changed earth? Recognizing species vulnerability in this larger biological sense is important to reducing false ideologies rooted in human exceptionalism. In *Timefulness: How Thinking Like a Geologist Can Help Save the World* (2018), Marcia Bjornerud attacks the idea of evolution as a progressive sequence culminating in *Homo sapiens*: "The great mass extinctions challenge any conceit that we are the triumphant culmination of 3.5 billion years of evolution. Life is always endlessly inventive, always tinkering and experimenting, but not with a particular notion of progress."[50] Confirming the legitimacy of the apocalyptic tradition's misanthropy,[51] Peter Brannen reviews the earth's past mass extinctions to conclude that "if humanity were to disappear tomorrow, the planet would quickly recover" although "the last thing to recover is biology."[52] In *The Selfish Ape: Human Nature and Our Path to Extinction* (2019), Nicholas Money explains that "we could not extinguish microbiology if we tried. With more

---

[48] David Abram, *Becoming Animal: An Earthly Cosmology* (New York: Pantheon Books, 2010), 290.
[49] Cormac McCarthy, *The Road* (New York: Vintage Books, 2006), 245. Subsequent citations appear parenthetically in the text.
[50] Cited in Verlyn Klinkenborg, "What Were Dinosaurs For?" *The New York Review of Books* LXVI, no. 20 (December 19, 2019): 34. Notice that Bjornerud's subtitle explicitly states that her purpose is to create massive social change to prevent climate catastrophe: she remains optimistic that such a thing is yet possible.
[51] See Andrew Tate, *Apocalyptic Fiction* (London: Bloomsbury Academic, 2017).
[52] Peter Brannen, *The Ends of the World: Volcanic Apocalypses, Lethal Oceans, and Our Quest to Understand Earth's Past Extinctions* (New York: Harper Collins, 2017), 243 and 274. Subsequent citations appear parenthetically in the text.

than 1 billion years of grace before the Sun starts glowing too bright, there is plenty of time for our home to be remade by the children of the evolutionary future."[53] What might the bacteria and blood sickness that decimate humans in *The Dogs Stars* evolve into? What might the hawks? Brannen speculates that "evolution will surely include some surprises" but

> Perhaps wild dogs, millions of years after reverting to wolves in the collapse of civilization, will take advantage of a landscape denuded of large herbivores and grow to the proportions of the gigantic Oligocene beast *Indricotherium* and grasp at tree branches towering overhead. Perhaps pigeons will chaperone us to our demise before growing to become 15-foot-tall flightless foragers. . . . Just as our lineage had to wait 200 million years after the Permian for another chance at the top, perhaps today's feathery descendants of dinosaurs will rule again in the next age. Of course this is wild speculation—the details will be filled in by the endlessly creative nonmind of evolution and happenstance. (275)

Something will evolve to fill the gaps, as something always has. In *A Friend of the Earth*, T.C. Boyle imagines rats "multiplying like there's no tomorrow (but of course there is, as everybody alive now knows all too well and ruefully, and tomorrow is coming for the rats too)."[54] Other species have evolved at the edges of our current lifeworld, including an Asian hornet, *Vespa orientalis*. They are scavengers of insect and animal proteins, nest underground, and use sound vibrations to communicate. In an ecocollapsed world, however, they are even more likely to survive because they are also the only known animal that "can operate, like a plant, directly on solar energy" by use of a photosynthetic organ on their abdomens.[55] *Vespa orientalis* already has flexible adaptations in place to enable its transition into and beyond the Anthropocene. I like to imagine huge colorful photosynthetic hornets becoming the earth's next charismatic megafauna.[56]

[53] Nicholas P. Money, *The Selfish Ape: Human Nature and Our Path to Extinction* (London: Reaktion Books, 2019), 20.
[54] T. C. Boyle, *A Friend of the Earth* (London: Bloomsbury, 2004), 6.
[55] Robert Bringhurst and Jan Zwicky, *Learning to Die: Wisdom in the Age of Climate Crisis* (Saskatchewan: University of Regina Press, 2018), 25.
[56] Although "huge" is a misnomer, because historically, insects were larger than they are today only in climates with higher levels of oxygen. Without additional adaptations, they will not grow in size amid the carbon dioxide levels anticipated in the later Anthropocene.

The realistic speculative fictions of ecocollapse analyzed in the previous chapters further hint toward what might flourish in the future. In *The Road*, the father smells "a lingering odor of cows in the barn and he stood there thinking about cows and he realized they were extinct" (120), unable to graze in the utterly devastated ecocollapsed landscape: large mammals are slowest to adapt to ecological change.[57] Standing at the edge of the "alien sea" (215), however, the father envisions "life in the deep. Great squid propelling themselves over the floor of the sea in the cold darkness. Shuttling past like trains, eyes the size of saucers" (219). With their complex neurological structures, perhaps cephalopods might adapt to reduced biodiversity, anoxic water, extreme temperatures, and other changing chemistries that accompany the complexity of climate change. It is true that rising ocean temperatures increase their growth and reproductive rates, but they are vulnerable to ocean acidification. Many of the world's oceans are currently experiencing increases in jellyfish populations, reminding us that the End-Permian mass extinction turned the acidic oceans into places with "a lot of green slime . . . and big blooms of jellyfish."[58] More likely is the survival of chemotrophs, microorganisms that already flourish around hydrothermal vents deep on the sea floor, adapted to the darkness by consuming sulfur, ammonia, iron, and hydrogen sulfide. Life in the deep ocean might be alien enough to survive anthropogenic transformations of the earth's surface and coastal seas.

Humans have gone extinct alongside the trout, elk, and some tree species in *The Dog Stars*, but the novel reveals that life itself will persevere. The environment adapts and rejuvenates, the silences "never silent but filled with birds, wren and lark. With the flashing wingbars of nighthawks at dusk. Later there were bat squeaks, the bustle of leaves, the sough of the lowering stream. All kinds of pastoral, a little strange given everything" (250). Even with "miles and miles of dead forest the spruce are coming back, the fir and the aspen" (295). Like McCarthy's *The Road*, which alludes to the survival of some unseen species in the depths of the ocean, Heller's novel reminds us that human extinction cannot prevent (and might even enable) the eventual flourishing

---

[57]   Nicholas Money forecasts that domestic cattle might be the largest surviving mammal in the Anthropocene because of their massive numbers (*The Selfish Ape*, 97).
[58]   Brannen, *Ends of the World*, 134.

of other life-forms on earth. The "Dry seedpods [that] scampered down the sands and stopped and then went on again" in *The Road* (McCarthy 216) might someday promulgate new life. Even a 32,000-year-old seed was found to be viable when it germinated in 2012.[59] In some form or another, life finds a way.

Just as human paleontologists today study the fossils of now-extinct species, whatever evolves in the climate changed future may study *Homo sapiens*, should they be so capable and so inclined. While fossils require quick burial in sedimentary rock to form, in Alan Weisman's forecast of *The World Without Us* he notes that "Polymers are forever."[60] Cultural artifacts like this book will decay and vanish, but humans have also created museums of *Homo sapiens* bodies that will last as long as the rest of the now-ubiquitous plastic: Gunther von Hagens's *Body Worlds* exhibition. Von Hagens constructs hundreds of elaborate, artful exhibits of human bodies and body parts using "plastination," his method of specimen preservation that solidifies the cadavers under vacuum by replacing body fluids with polymers. As he describes the process in the exhibit book, "Plastination creates beautiful specimens as a sensuous experience that are frozen at a point between death and decay."[61] Like taxidermized nonhuman animals, the plastinated human mounts are set in frozen action: a man on his knees gives chest compressions to another; one man stands proudly with his arm raised, his own skin hanging across it like a coat; a reclining pregnant woman with her fetus exposed poses like Giorgione's *The Sleeping Venus*. Some specimens are displayed to expose the musculature, vascular, or nervous system; others are separated into organs and other body part configurations; still others are fixed into complex dioramas reminiscent of the posed displays in the Hall of Mammals at the United States National Museum of Natural History. At the Great Exhibition in 1851 in London, Herman Ploucquet exhibited mounted animals anthropomorphically in scenes where the taxidermied animal mounts were "engaged in performing human occupations, and seemingly influenced by human motives, hopes, and fears."[62]

[59] See Rachel Kaufman, "32000-Year-Old Plant Brought Back to Life—Oldest Yet," *National Geographic News*, February 21, 2012.
[60] Alan Weisman, *The World Without Us* (New York: Thomas Dunne Books, 2007), Chapter 9.
[61] Gunther von Hagens and Angelina Whalley, *The Anatomical Exhibition of Real Human Bodies* (Heidelberg: Institute for Plastination, 2004), 20.
[62] From the *Morning Chronicle*, August 12, 1851, quoted in Poliquin, *The Breathless Zoo: Taxidermy and the Cultures of Longing* (University Park: Pennsylvania State University Press, 2012), 176.

Taxidermy has a long history with its origins in the preservation of animal skins for clothing and upholstery but evolved into the techniques seen today in the natural history collections popular at the turn of the nineteenth century because "Desire," Rachel Poliquin writes, "creates its objects: taxidermied animals are not naturally occurring. . . . It is the animal itself that activates, substantiates, and perpetuates human craving for its vitality and form."[63] In *Body Worlds*, however, the viewer finds a distinctly human animal as vital object. The *Body Worlds* exhibits thus function, to use the words of Jane Bennett, "to present human and nonhuman actants on a less vertical plane"[64] in a near-permanent way, available for the study by any future species so capable.

Once again, human exceptionalism makes the "thingness" of plastinated human mounts difficult to accept, made most obvious in ways relevant to the origins of the dead body itself. For example, there are legal differences between the anatomical specimens of scientific enterprise and decaying human corpses: anatomical studies are used for instruction and medical cadavers are anonymous to preserve privacy; corpses are objects of mourning subject to burial laws and rites that indicate grieving and are explicitly named for their person, except in circumstances where a corpse cannot be identified. Property and privacy laws apply on the one hand while burial laws on the other. Similarly, the various *Body Worlds* exhibits are not without ethical complexity. In the case of human bodies, one controversy is related to proving the once-living human's consent to being plastinated and publicly displayed. Von Hagens has been inundated with questions about how cadavers were acquired, particularly those with origins in nations with documented human rights violations. As he puts it, "Critics have repeatedly claimed that the exhibition includes specimens from people who would never have wanted to go on display."[65] The plastinated mounts are clearly labeled with signs indicating that all anatomical displays' human bodies originate from the Body Donation Program he established and that the human specimens exhibited

---

[63]   Poliquin, *The Breathless Zoo*, 8.

[64]   Jane Bennett, *Vibrant Matter: A Political Ecology of Things* (Durham, NC: Duke University Press, 2010), ix.

[65]   Gunther von Hagens, "No Skeletons in the Closet: Facts, Background and Conclusions," *Body Worlds*, November 17, 2003, 3. bodyworlds.com/Downloads/E_Kirgisien%20AW%20GVH%202. pdf.

are properly acquired with explicit consent. In contrast, in the case of the nonhuman bodies he also plastinates and puts on display, the controversy is one of potential animal abuse. Other animals are assumed unable to give consent, so their exhibits are labeled instead with notices indicating that "No animal was harmed or killed for use in this exhibition." Interestingly, when von Hagens suspected some human corpses were unclaimed or otherwise did not purposefully consent, he directed that they be cremated, shifting their thingness back from scientific object to human personhood.[66] In other words, human exceptionalism extends even to the thing a human body becomes when dead.

The plastinated figures themselves, however, are a fascinating juxtaposition of anatomical specimen, contemporary art, a desperate attempt to immortalize the human species, and the phenomena of the human animal body exposed for intimate observation, what von Hagens calls the "sensuous experience." The corpse is not simply preserved for study but is shaped into colorful, visually disorienting displays: bodily materiality of an entirely different sort than the kind Stacy Alaimo articulates. "All taxidermy," Rachel Poliquin writes, "is a disorienting, unknowable thing. All taxidermy is driven to capture animal beauty. It is always a spectacle whose meaning depends in part on the particularity of the animal being displayed. It is motivated by the desire to tell ourselves stories about who we are and about our journey within the larger social and natural world."[67] Part of this storytelling seems to arise from wonder at being in the presence of such a familiar kind of being, yet part of the creative spirit seems vulgar—an uncomfortable ghoulishness, perhaps— because the plastinated human was but is no longer alive. Both taxidermy and plastination make a thing from a living being, and the wonder viewers experience is not because the body is dead; the wonder comes from the

---

[66] *Body Worlds* is easily confused with a similar exhibition created by von Hagens's former employee called *Bodies: The Exhibition*, which openly acknowledges that the exhibit displays full-body mounts as well as human body parts, organs, fetuses, and embryos that come from cadavers of Chinese citizens or residents who were likely executed while incarcerated in Chinese prisons. Their website disclaimer states that the displayed humans died from natural causes and were unclaimed at death (see bodiestheexhibition.com/faq.html). While my purpose in this thought exercise is not to explore the injustice of these exhibits but to imagine how they might long outlast humans on earth, the lack of agency available to those presumed less-than-human is another haunting way in which inequitable privilege and othering has unjust consequences in the present day.

[67] Poliquin, *The Breathless Zoo*, 7.

knowledge that the mounted object once lived. As Poliquin asks, "What does it mean to be dead but not gone?"[68] Taxidermized mounts will not survive the thousands of years' time needed for any future species' development into a creature able to ponder their existence, but plastinated bodies just might, so the longing Poliquin describes as taxidermy's motivations are useful to ponder. Poliquin lists seven: wonder, beauty, spectacle, order, narrative, allegory, and remembrance, and she says that these incentives function as "a mechanism for both pacifying and cultivating various lusts and hungers by creating objects capable of generating significance."[69] Here too, remembrance performs both symbolic and literal functions amid human extinction, one that might enable a species far in the future to wonder about what we once were, plastic becoming minerals in the fossils of humankind.

Humans may be the most charismatic of the charismatic megafauna, but as this book has shown, human exceptionalism does not hold up amid cultures of human extinction. Cary Wolfe observes that "there is nothing more 'natural' than extinction."[70] Our shared animality entangles humans with the more-than-human world in ways that reveal that our supposedly "moral" cultural and social structures are always falsely durable and that our bodily corporeality is always interconnected with material incorporation. Biodiversity loss results in a cannibalism of any residue of what makes us "human." As Ursula K. Heise puts it, "Human beings destroy habitats to survive themselves."[71] A less-subtle manifestation is the contemplation that my calf muscle might go well with chickweed and ivy, roasted slowly over a campfire or dried to jerky in the sun, the sounds of drumming in the distance or the slow knocking of waves or just in eerie silence, nourishing whatever hungry being happens by, perhaps even the Covid-19 virus while it replicates beyond my body's capacity to manage. The characters in these fictions variously take the measure of their own insignificance as part of the tangled webs of ecosystems and lineages shaping each other, demonstrating the contingencies of this ecological moment. One

---

[68] Ibid., 9.
[69] Ibid., 7.
[70] Cary Wolfe, "Condors at the End of the World," in *After Extinction*, ed. Richard Grusin (Minnesota: University of Minnesota Press, 2018), 107.
[71] Ursula K. Heise, *Imagining Extinction: The Cultural Meanings of Endangered Species* (Chicago, IL: University of Chicago Press, 2016), 28.

day we will not exist. How do we deal with that fact? Rather than clinging to human exceptionalism, we might use our imaginations to stay with the trouble and envision the future without humans in it so as to come to terms with the failures of human exceptionalism, to accept impermanence, and to engage from worldviews in which we are equal members likewise in perpetual change.

Bibliography

Abram, David. *Becoming Animal: An Earthly Cosmology.* New York: Pantheon Books, 2010.

Adams, Carol. *The Sexual Politics of Meat: A Feminist-Vegetarian Critical Theory.* New York: Continuum Publishing, 1996.

Agamben, Giorgio. *The Open: Man and Animal,* translated by Kevin Attell. Stanford: Stanford University Press, 2004.

Alaimo, Stacy. *Bodily Natures: Science, Environment, and the Material Self.* Bloomington: Indiana University Press, 2010.

Alaimo, Stacy. *Exposed: Environmental Politics and Pleasures in Posthuman Times.* Minneapolis: University of Minnesota Press, 2016.

Alaimo, Stacy. "Sustainable This, Sustainable That: New Materialisms, Posthumanism and Unknown Futures." *PMLA* 127, no. 3 (2012): 558–64.

Alaimo, Stacy, and Susan J. Hekman, eds. *Material Feminisms.* Bloomington: Indiana University Press, 2007.

Alexander, Kurtis. "Pilots 'Seed' Clouds, Fighting the Drought from the Sky." *The San Francisco Chronicle,* April 3, 2016.

Anderson, Gregers. "Cli-Fi and the Uncanny." *ISLE: Interdisciplinary Studies in Literature and the Environment* 23, no. 4 (Autumn 2016): 855–66.

Armstrong, Phillip. *What Animals Mean in the Fiction of Modernity.* New York: Routledge, 2008.

Atwood, Margaret. *In Other Worlds: SF and the Human Imagination.* London: Doubleday, 2011.

Baker, Carolyn. *Love in the Age of Ecological Apocalypse.* Berkeley, CA: North Atlantic Books, 2015.

Bakhtin, Mikhail. *The Dialogic Imagination: Four Essays,* translated by Caryl Emerson and Michael Holquist. Austin: University of Texas Press, 1983.

Barad, Karen. *Meeting the Universe Halfway: Quantum Physics and the Entanglement of Matter and Meaning.* Durham, NC: Duke University Press, 2007.

Barad, Karen. "Posthumanist Performativity: Toward an Understanding of How Matter Comes to Matter." *Signs: Journal of Women in Culture and Society* 28, no. 3 (2003): 801–31.

Bartky, Sandra Lee. *Femininity and Domination: Studies in the Phenomenology of Oppression.* New York: Routledge, 1990.

Beck, Ulrich. *World at Risk*, translated by Ciaran Cronin. Cambridge: Polity, 2009.

Bellamy, Brent Ryan. "The Reproductive Imperative of *The Road.*" *The Cormac McCarthy Journal* 16, no. 1 (2018): 38–54.

Bendell, Jem. "Deep Adaptation: A Map for Navigating Climate Tragedy." *IFLAS Occasional Paper* 2 (July 27, 2018). PDF: https://www.lifeworth.com/deepadaptation.pdf.

Benjamin, Walter. "Critique of Violence." In *Selected Writings: 1913–1926 Volume 1*, edited and translated by Marcus Paul Bullock, Michael William Jennings, and Howard Eiland, 236–52. Boston, MA: Harvard University Press, 1996.

Bennett, Jane. *Vibrant Matter: A Political Ecology of Things*. Durham, NC: Duke University Press, 2010.

Berger, John. "Why Look at Animals?" In *About Looking*, 3–28. New York: Vintage Books, 1980.

Berger, John. *Why Look at Animals?* London: Penguin, 2009.

Berlant, Lauren. *Cruel Optimism*. Durham, NC: Duke University Press, 2011.

Bjornerud, Marcia. *Timefulness: How Thinking Like a Geologist Can Help Save the World*. Princeton, NJ: Princeton University Press, 2018.

Boyle, T. C. *A Friend of the Earth*. London: Bloomsbury, 2004.

Bradford, Alina. "Sloths: The World's Slowest Animals." *Live Science*, November 26, 2018. https://livescience.com/27612-sloths.html.

Brannen, Peter. *The Ends of the World: Volcanic Apocalypses, Lethal Oceans, and Our Quest to Understand Earth's Past Extinctions*. New York: Harper Collins, 2017.

Bringhurst, Robert, and Jan Zwicky. *Learning to Die: Wisdom in the Age of Climate Crisis*. Saskatchewan: University of Regina Press, 2018.

Brownmiller, Susan. *Against Our Will: Men, Women, and Rape*. New York: Ballentine Books, 1975.

Bruneau, Emile, Mina Cikara, and Rebecca Saxe. "Parochial Empathy Predicts Reduced Altruism and the Endorsement of Passive Harm." *Journal of Social Psychology and Personality Science* 8, no. 8 (June 2017): 934–42.

Buber, Martin. *I and Thou*. New York: Scribner, 1958.

Burnett, Lucy. "What If: The Literary Case for More Climate Change." *ISLE: Interdisciplinary Studies in Literature and Environment* 26, no. 4 (Autumn 2019): 901–23.

Butler, Judith. *Precarious Life: The Powers of Mourning and Violence*. London: Verso, 2004.

Butler, Judith. *Senses of the Subject*. New York: Fordham University Press, 2015.

Butler, Octavia E. *Parable of the Sower*. New York: Grand Central Publishing, 1993.

Cahill, Ann J. *Rethinking Rape*. Ithaca: Cornell University Press, 2001.

Chakrabarty, Dipesh. "The Climate of History: Four Theses." *Critical Inquiry* 35, no. 2 (Winter 2009): 197–222.

Cheuse, Alan. "'The Dog Stars' by Peter Heller." Book Review. *The Boston Globe*. August 15, 2012. https://www.bostonglobe.com/arts/books/2012/08/15/review-book-the-dog-stars-peter-heller/UxjqQFMxrmfDxVMjbrtHYO/story.html.

Childs, Craig. *Apocalyptic Planet: A Field Guide to the Future of the Earth*. New York: Vintage Books, 2013.

Christensen, Nels Anchor. "Facing the Weather in James Galvin's *The Meadow* and Cormac McCarthy's *The Road*." *ISLE: Interdisciplinary Studies in Literature and Environment* 21, no. 1 (Winter 2014): 192–204.

Clare, Eli. "Meditations on Natural Worlds, Disabled Bodies, and a Politics of Cure." In *Material Ecocriticism*, edited by Serenella Iovino and Serpil Oppermann, 204–18. Bloomington: University of Indiana Press, 2014.

Clark, Timothy. *Ecocriticism on the Edge: The Anthropocene as a Threshold Concept*. London: Bloomsbury Academic, 2015.

Connolly, William E. "Extinction Events and Entangled Humanism." In *After Extinction*, edited by Richard Grusin, 1–26. Minneapolis: University of Minnesota Press, 2018.

Coogan, Michael D., ed. *The New Oxford Annotated Bible*. 3rd ed. Oxford: Oxford University Press, 2001.

Cribb, Julian. *The Coming Famine: The Global Food Crisis and What We Can Do About It*. Berkeley: University of California Press, 2010.

Curtis, Claire P. *Postapocalyptic Fiction and the Social Contract: "We'll Not Go Home Again."* Lanham, MD: Lexington Books, 2010.

DeBruyn, Ben. "The Hot War: Climate, Security, Fiction." *Studies in the Novel* 50, no. 1 (Spring 2018): 43–67.

DeCoste, D. Marcel. "'A Thing That Even Death Cannot Undo': The Operation of The Theological Virtues in Cormac McCarthy's *The Road*." *Religion and Literature Journal* 44, no. 2 (Summer 2012): 67–91.

DeFleur, Alban, Tim White, Patricia Valensi, Ludovic Slimak, and Evelyne Cregut-Bonnoure. "Neanderthal Cannibalism at Moula-Guercy, Ardeche, France." *Science* 286, no. 5437 (November 1999): 128–31. doi: 10.1126/science.286.5437.128.

Dennis, Brady, and Andrew Freedman. "Here's How the Hottest Month in Recorded History Unfolded Around the World." *The Washington Post*, August 5, 2019.

Derrida, Jacques. "The Animal That Therefore I Am (More to Follow)." In *The Animal That Therefore I Am*, edited by Marie-Louise Mallet and translated by David Wills, 1–51. New York: Fordham University Press, 2008.

Derrida, Jacques. "'Eating Well', Or the Calculation of the Subject: An Interview with Jacques Derrida." In *Who Comes after the Subject?*, edited by Eduardo Cadava, Peter Connor, and Jean-Luc Nancy, 96–119. New York: Routledge, 1991.

Derrida, Jacques. "The Principle of Hospitality." *Angelaka* 5, no. 3 (2005): 6–9.

Duncan, Heather, and Eleanor Gold. "Abject Permanence: Apocalyptic Narratives and the Horror of Persistence." In *Green Matters: Ecocultural Functions of Literature*, edited by Maria Loschnigg and Melanie Braunecker, 201–16. Leiden, The Netherlands: Brill, 2019.

Duncan, Rebecca. "*Life of Pi* as Postmodern Survivor Narrative." *Mosaic: An Interdisciplinary Critical Journal* 41, no. 2 (June 2008): 167–83.

Ehrlich, Paul, and Anne Ehrlich. *One with Ninevah: Politics, Consumption, and the Human Future*. Washington, DC: Island Press, 2004.

Elliott, Jane. "Suffering Agency: Imagining Neoliberal Personhood in North America and Britain." *Social Text* (115) 31, no. 2 (Summer 2013): 83–101.

Erdrich, Louise. *Future Home of the Living God: A Novel*. New York: HarperCollins Publishers, 2017.

Fagan, Madeleine. "Who's Afraid of the Ecological Apocalypse? Climate Change and the Production of the Ethical Subject." *The British Journal of Politics and International Relations* 19, no. 2 (2017): 225–44.

Fiskio, Janet. "Apocalypse and Ecotopia: Narratives in Global Climate Change Discourse." *Race, Gender & Class* 19, nos. 1–2 (2012): 12–36.

Forna, Aminatta. *The Memory of Love*. London: Bloomsbury, 2011.

Fox-Skelly, Jasmin. "There Are Diseases Hidden in Ice, and They Are Waking Up." *BBC Earth*, May 4, 2017. bbc.com/earth/story/20170504-there-are-diseases-hidden-in-ice-and-they-are-waking-up.

Fraiman, Susan. "Pussy Panic versus Liking Animals: Tracking Gender in Animal Studies." *Critical Inquiry* 39 (Autumn 2012): 89–115.

Francis, Richard C. *Domesticated: Evolution in a Man-made World*. New York: Norton, 2015.

Gardner, Claire. "The Apocalypse Is Easy: Limitations of Our Climate Change Imaginings." *Demos*, September 13, 2015.

Garforth, Lisa. "Green Utopias: Beyond Apocalypse, Progress, and Pastoral." *Utopian Studies* 16, no. 3 (2005): 393–427.

Garrard, Greg. "Worlds Without Us: Some Types of Disanthropy." *SubStance* 41 (2012): 40–60.

Gawande, Atul. *Being Mortal: Medicine and What Matters at the End*. New York: Picador, 2014.

Ghosh, Amitav. *The Great Derangement: Climate Change and the Unthinkable*. Chicago, IL: University of Chicago Press, 2017.

Ghosh, Amitav. *The Hungry Tide*. Boston, MA: Houghton Mifflin Harcourt, 2006.

Gilbert, Chris. "The Quest of a Father and Son: Illuminating Character Identity, Motivation, and Conflict in Cormac McCarthy's *The Road*." *English Journal* 102, no. 1 (2012): 40–7.

Gleick, Peter H. "Water, Drought, Climate Change, and Conflict in Syria." *American Meteorological Society* 6 (July 2014): 331–40.

Greenberg, David M., Simon Baron-Cohen, Nora Rosenberg, Peter Fonagy, and Peter J. Rentfrow. "Elevated Empathy in Adults Following Childhood Trauma." *PLoS One* 13, no. 10 (October 2, 2018). doi: 10.1371/journal.pone.0203886.

Grusin, Richard, ed. *After Extinction*. Minneapolis: University of Minnesota Press, 2018.

Guterl, Fred. *The Fate of the Species: Why the Human Race May Cause Its Own Extinction and How We Can Stop It*. London: Bloomsbury, 2013.

Hamilton, Clive. *Requiem for a Species: Why We Resist the Truth about Climate Change*. London: Earthscan, 2010.

Hamilton, Geoff. "Something to Be Done: *The Road*, Beckett, and American Autonomy." *Canadian Review of American Studies* 47, no. 1 (2017): 54–75.

Hansen, James, Makiko Sato, Pushker Kharecha, David Beerling, Robert Berner, Valerie Masson-Delmotte, Mark Pagani, et al. "Target Atmospheric CO_2: Where Should Humanity Aim?" *Open Atmospheric Science Journal* 2 (2008): 217–31.

Haraway, Donna J. *The Companion Species Manifesto: Dogs, People, and Significant Otherness*. Chicago, IL: Prickly Paradigm, 2003.

Haraway, Donna J. *Simians, Cyborgs and Women: The Reinvention of Nature*. New York: Routledge, 1991.

Haraway, Donna J. *Staying with the Trouble: Making Kin in the Chthulucene*. Durham, NC: Duke University Press, 2016.

Haraway, Donna J. *When Species Meet*. Minneapolis: University of Minnesota Press, 2008.

Harris, Marvin. *Cannibals and Kings: The Origins of Cultures*. New York: Random House, 1977.

Hegland, Jean. *Into the Forest*. New York: Dial Press, 1998.

Heise, Ursula K. *Imagining Extinction: The Cultural Meanings of Endangered Species*. Chicago, IL: Chicago University Press, 2016.

Heller, Peter. *The Dog Stars*. New York: Vintage Books, 2012.

Hertsgaard, Mark. *Hot: Living Through the Next Fifty Years on Earth*. New York: Houghton Mifflin Harcourt, 2011.

Hoberek, Andrew. "Cormac McCarthy and the Aesthetics of Exhaustion." *American Literary History* 23, no. 3 (July 2011): 483–99.

Hochschild, Arlie Russell. *Strangers in Their Own Land: Anger and Mourning on the American Right*. New York: The New Press, 2016.

Huggan, Graham, and Helen Tiffin. *Postcolonial Ecocriticism: Literature, Animals, Environment*. New York: Routledge, 2010.

Hughes, Rowland, and Pat Wheeler. "Eco-dystopias: Nature and the Dystopian Imagination." *Critical Survey* 25, no. 2 (2013): 1–6.

Hume, Clara. *Back to the Garden*. California: Moon Willow Press, 2013.

Iovene, Paola. *Tales of Futures Past: Anticipation and the Ends of Literature in Contemporary China*. Stanford, CA: Stanford University Press, 2014.

Iovino, Serenella. "Restoring the Imagination of Place: Narrative Reinhabitation and the Po Valley." In *The Bioregional Imagination: Literature, Ecology, and Place*, edited by Tom Lynch, Cheryll Glotfelty, and Karla Armbruster, 100–17. Athens: University of Georgia Press, 2010.

Johns-Putra, Adeline. "'My Job Is to Take Care of You': Climate Change, Humanity, and Cormac McCarthy's *The Road*." *Modern Fiction Studies* 62, no. 3 (Fall 2016): 519–40.

Johns-Putra, Adeline. "The Rest Is Silence: Postmodern and Postcolonial Possibilities in Climate Change Fiction." *Studies in the Novel* 50, no. 1 (Spring 2018): 26–42.

Johns-Putra, Adeline, John Parham, and Louise Squire, eds. *Literature and Sustainability: Concept, Text and Culture*. Manchester: Manchester University Press, 2017.

Junger, Sebastian. *Tribe: On Homecoming and Belonging*. New York: Twelve Hachette Books, 2016.

Kaplan, E. Ann. *Climate Trauma: Foreseeing the Future in Dystopian Film*. New Jersey: Rutgers University Press, 2016.

Kaufman, Rachel. "32000-Year-Old Plant Brought Back to Life—Oldest Yet." *National Geographic News*, February 21, 2012.

Kerridge, Richard. "The Single Source." *Ecozon@* 1, no. 1 (2010): 155–61. doi: 10.37536/ECOZONA.2010.1.1.334.

Kilgour, Maggie. *From Communion to Cannibalism: An Anatomy of Metaphors of Incorporation*. Princeton, NJ: Princeton University Press, 1990.

King, Stephen. *The Stand: The Complete and Uncut Version*. 1990. Expanded reprint. New York: Anchor Books, 2011.

Kintisch, Eli. "'Asilomar 2' Takes Small Steps Toward Rules for Geoengineering." *Science* 328, no. 5974 (April 2, 2010): 22–3.

Klein, Naomi. *On Fire: The Burning Case for a Green New Deal*. New York: Simon and Schuster, 2019.

Klinkenborg, Verlyn. "What Were Dinosaurs For?" *The New York Review of Books* 66, no. 20 (December 19, 2019): 34–8.

Knox, Paul D. "'Okay Means Okay': Ideology and Survival in Cormac McCarthy's *The Road*." *The Explicator* 70, no. 2 (2012): 96–9.

Kolbert, Elizabeth. *Field Notes from a Catastrophe: Man, Nature, and Climate Change*. New York: Bloomsbury USA, 2006.

Kunsa, Ashley. "'Maps of the World in Its Becoming': Post-Apocalyptic Naming in Cormac McCarthy's *The Road*." *Journal of Modern Literature* 33, no. 1 (Fall 2009): 57–74.

LeMenager, Stephanie. "Climate Change and the Struggle for Genre." In *Anthropocene Reading: Literary History in Geologic Times*, edited by Tobias Menely and Jesse Oak Taylor, 220–38. University Park: Pennsylvania State University Press, 2017.

Levinas, Emmanuel. *Totality and Infinity*, translated by A. Lingis. Pittsburgh, PA: Duquesne University Press, 1969.

Lincoln, Kenneth. *Cormac McCarthy*. New York: Palgrave, 2009.

Lozier, Lynn. "Flying Over the Future." Review of *The Dog Stars*, by Peter Heller. *Science Chronicles Mid-Year Books Issue*, June 2013.

Lukes, Steven. *Moral Relativism*. London: Picador, 2008.

MacFarlane, Robert. Introduction to *The Crystal World*, by J. G. Ballard, xi–xvi. Reprint. New York: Picador, 2018.

Magistrale, Tony. "Free Will and Sexual Choice in *The Stand*." *Extrapolation* 34, no. 1 (1993): 30–8.

Malamud, Randy. *Reading Zoos: Representations of Animals and Captivity*. New York: New York University Press, 1998.

Mandel, Emily St. John. *Station Eleven*. New York: Vintage Press, 2014.

Margulis, Lynn. *Symbiotic Planet: A New Look at Evolution*. New York: Basic Books, 1998.

Marshall, George. *Don't Even Think about It: Why Our Brains Are Wired to Ignore Climate Change*. London: Bloomsbury, 2014.

Martel, Yann. *Life of Pi: A Novel*. Orlando, FL: Harcourt, 2001.

Martin, Mark, ed. *I'm with the Bears: Short Stories from a Damaged Planet*. New York: Verso, 2011.

McCarthy, Cormac. *The Road*. New York: Vintage Books, 2006.

McCarthy, Terry. "Japanese Troops 'Ate Flesh of Enemies and Civilians'." *The Independent*, August 12, 1992.

McFarland, Sarah E. "Animal Studies, Literary Animals, and Yann Martel's *Life of Pi*." In *The Cambridge Companion to Literature and the Environment*, edited by Louise Westling, 152–65. New York: Cambridge University Press, 2014.

McFarland, Sarah E. "'Just Meat on Legs': The Last Stragglers of Climate Apocalypse." *ISLE: Interdisciplinary Studies in Literature and Environment* 26, no. 4 (Autumn 2019): 864–81.

McFarland, Sarah E. "Such 'Beastly' Behavior! Predation, Revenge, and the Question of Ethics." In *Exploring Animal Encounters: Philosophical, Cultural, and Historical Perspectives*, edited by Dominik Ohrem and Matthew Calarco, 93–111. London: Palgrave Macmillan, 2018.

McKibben, Bill. *Eaarth: Making a Life on a Tough New Planet*. New York: Henry Holt, 2010.

McKibben, Bill. *Falter: Has the Human Game Begun to Play Itself Out?* New York: Henry Holt, 2019.

McKibben, Bill. "Global Warming's Terrifying New Math." *Rolling Stone Magazine*, July 19, 2012.

McKibben, Bill. Introduction to *I'm with the Bears: Short Stories from a Damaged Planet*, edited by Mark Martin, 1–5. London: Verso, 2011.

Mead, Simon, Michael P. H. Stumpf, Jerome Whitfield, Jonathan A. Beck, Mark Poulter, Tracy Campbell, James B. Uphill, et al. "Balancing Selection at the Prion Protein Gene Consistent with Prehistoric Kurulike Epidemics." *Science* 300, no. 5691 (April 25, 2003): 640–3. doi: 10.1126/science.1083320.

Mehnert, Antonia. *Climate Change Fictions: Representations of Global Warming in American Literature*. Switzerland: Palgrave Macmillan, 2016.

Mehta, Suketu. *This Land Is Our Land: An Immigrant's Manifesto*. New York: Farrar, Straus and Giroux, 2019.

Mehta, Ved. "The New India of Indira Gandhi." *The New Yorker*, February 14, 1977.

Menely, Tobias, and Jesse Oak Taylor, eds. *Anthropocene Reading: Literary History in Geologic Times*. University Park: Pennsylvania State University Press, 2017.

Mirzoeff, Nicholas. "It's Not the Anthropocene, It's the White Supremacy Scene; or, The Geological Color Line." In *After Extinction*, edited by Richard Grusin, 123–49. Minneapolis: University of Minnesota Press, 2018.

Monbiot, George. "Civilization Ends with a Shutdown of Human Concern. Are We There Already?" *The Guardian*, October 30, 2007.

Money, Nicholas P. *The Selfish Ape: Human Nature and Our Path to Extinction*. London: Reaktion Books, 2019.

Montaigne, Michel de. "Of Cannibals." In *The Essays of Michel de Montaigne*, vol. 1, translated by Jacob Zeitlin, 178–90. New York: Knopf, 1934.

Moore, Kathleen Dean, and Scott Slovic. "A Call to Writers." *ISLE: Interdisciplinary Studies in Literature and Environment* 21, no. 1 (Winter 2014): 5–8.

Morgenstern, Naomi. "Postapocalyptic Responsibility: Patriarchy at the End of the World in Cormac McCarthy's *The Road*." *Differences: A Journal of Feminist Cultural Studies* 25, no. 2 (Summer 2014): 33–61.

Mortimer-Sandilands, Catriona. "Melancholy Natures, Queer Ecologies." In *Queer Ecologies: Sex, Nature, Politics, Desire*, edited by Mortimer-Sandilands and Bruce Erickson, 331–58. Bloomington: Indiana University Press, 2010.

Morton, Timothy. *Being Ecological*. Cambridge, MA: MIT Press, 2018.

Mullan, Robert, and Gary Marvin. *Zoo Culture: The Book about Watching People Watch Animals*. 2nd ed. Urbana: University of Illinois Press, 1998.

Nagel, Thomas. "What Is It Like to Be a Bat?" *Philosophical Review* 83, no. 4 (October 1974): 435–50.

NASA. "2016 Arctic Sea Ice Wintertime Extent Hits Another Record Low," March 28, 2016. http://www.nasa.gov/feature/goddard/2016/2016-arctic-sea-ice-wintertime-extent-hits-another-record-low.

NASA/GISS. "Global Land-Ocean Temperature Index," 2019. https://data.giss.nasa.gov/gistemp/.

National Research Council (United States National Academies of Sciences, Engineering, Medicine). *Climate Intervention: Carbon Dioxide Removal and Reliable Sequestration*. Washington, DC: The National Academies Press, 2015. https://doi.org/10.17226/18805.

National Research Council (United States National Academies of Sciences, Engineering, Medicine). *Climate Intervention: Reflecting Sunlight to Cool Earth*. Washington, DC: The National Academies Press, 2015. https://doi.org/10.17226/18988.

Nayar, Pramod K. *Ecoprecarity: Vulnerable Lives in Literature and Culture*. New York: Routledge, 2019.

News.com.au. "Pumice Raft Bigger than Area of Israel." August 10, 2012. http://www.news.com.au/world/breaking-news/undersea-eruption-creates-pumic-raft/news-story/C2e7dd297df3546e605b0c72b4dc4a2f.

Nixon, Rob. *Slow Violence and the Environmentalism of the Poor*. Cambridge, MA: Harvard University Press, 2011.

Nordhaus, Ted, and Michael Shellenberger. "Apocalypse Fatigue: Losing the Public on Climate Change." *Yale Environment 360*, November 16, 2009.

Oreskes, Naomi, and Eric M. Conway. *The Collapse of Western Civilization: A View from the Future*. New York: Columbia University Press, 2014.

Owen, Stephen. *The Late Tang: Chinese Poetry of the Mid-Ninth Century (827–860)*. Cambridge, MA: Harvard University Press, 2006.

Oxfam International. "Forced from Home: Climate-Fueled Displacement." December 2, 2019.

Patton, Paul. "McCarthy's Fire." In *Styles of Extinction: Cormac McCarthy's The Road*, edited by Julian Murphet and Mark Steven, 131–43. New York: Continuum Publishing, 2013.

Pilkey, Orrin H., and Rob Young. *The Rising Sea*. Washington, DC: Island Press, 2009.

Pilkey, Orrin H., Linda Pilkey-Jarvis, and Keith C. Pilkey. *Retreat from a Rising Sea: Hard Choices in an Age of Climate Change*. New York: Columbia University Press, 2017.

Poliquin, Rachel. *The Breathless Zoo: Taxidermy and the Cultures of Longing*. University Park: Pennsylvania State University Press, 2012.

Quammen, David. *The Song of the Dodo: Island Biogeography in an Age of Extinctions*. New York: Scribner, 1996.

Raboteau, Emily. "Lessons in Survival." *The New York Review of Books* 66, no. 18 (November 21, 2019): 13–15.

Rambo, Shelly L. "Beyond Redemption? Reading Cormac McCarthy's *The Road* After the End of the World." *Studies in the Literary Imagination* 41, no. 2 (Fall 2008): 99–120.

Ray, Sarah Jaquette. *A Field Guide to Climate Anxiety: How to Keep Your Cool on a Warming Planet*. Berkeley: University of California Press, 2020.

Read, Piers Paul. *Alive: The Story of the Andes Survivors*. New York: HarperCollins, 1975.

Redfield, Robert. *Human Nature and the Study of Society: The Papers of Robert Redfield*, edited by Margaret P. Redfield. Chicago, IL: Chicago University Press, 1962.

Reese, Jennifer. "'Dog Stars' Dwells on the Upside of Apocalypse." Review of *The Dog Stars*, by Peter Heller. *NPR Books*. August 7, 2012.

Rexroth, Kenneth. *One Hundred More Poems from the Chinese: Love and the Turning Year*. New York: New Directions Publishing, 1970.

Rigby, Kate. *Dancing with Disaster: Environmental Histories, Narratives, and Ethics for Perilous Times*. Charlottesville: University of Virginia Press, 2015.

Rose, Deborah Bird. *Wild Dog Dreaming*. Charlottesville: University of Virginia Press, 2011.

Royal Society. "Geoengineering the Climate: Science, Governance, and Uncertainty." September 1, 2009. PDF: https://eprints.soton.ac.uk/156647/.

Sanday, Peggy Reeves. *Divine Hunger: Cannibalism as a Cultural System*. Cambridge, MA: Cambridge University Press, 1986.

Sapolsky, Robert M. *Behave: The Biology of Humans at Our Best and Worst*. New York: Penguin Books, 2017.

Schaub, Thomas H. "Secular Scripture and Cormac McCarthy's *The Road*." *Renascence* 61, no. 3 (Spring 2009): 153–68.

Schneider-Mayerson, Matthew. "Climate Change Fiction." In *American Literature in Transition, 2000–2010*, edited by Rachel Greenwald Smith, 309–21. Cambridge, MA: Cambridge University Press, 2017.

Schutt, Bill. *Cannibalism: A Perfectly Natural History*. Chapel Hill, NC: Algonquin Books, 2017.

Scranton, Roy. *Learning to Die in the Anthropocene: Reflections on the End of a Civilization*. San Francisco, CA: City Lights Books, 2015.

Seabrook, William Bueller. *Jungle Ways*. London: George G. Harrap, 1931.

Seymour, Nicole. *Strange Natures: Futurity, Empathy, and the Queer Ecological Imagination*. Chicago: University of Illinois Press, 2013.

Shotwell, Alexis. *Against Purity: Living Ethically in Compromised Times*. Minneapolis: University of Minnesota Press, 2016.

Simpson, Helen. "Diary of an Interesting Year." In *In-Flight Entertainment: Stories*, 144–59. New York: Alfred A. Knopf, 2012.

Skrimshire, Stefan. "'There Is No God and We Are His Prophets': Deconstructing Redemption in Cormac McCarthy's *The Road*." *Journal for Cultural Research* 15, no. 1 (January 2011): 1–14.

Smith, Zadie. "Elegy for a Country's Seasons." *The New York Review of Books* 61, no. 6 (April 3, 2014): 6.

Snowpiercer. Directed by Bong Joon-ho. South Korea: Moho Film, 2013.

Softing, Inger-Anne. "Between Dystopia and Utopia: The Post-Apocalyptic Discourse of Cormac McCarthy's *The Road*." *English Studies* 94, no. 6 (2013): 704–13.

Solnit, Rebecca. *A Paradise Built in Hell: The Extraordinary Communities That Arise in Disaster*. New York: Viking, 2009.

Sontag, Susan. "The Imagination of Disaster." In *Against Interpretation and Other Essays*, 209–25. New York: Dell Publishing, 1979.

Spencer, Geoff. "Japan Hears of World War II Cannibalism a Half-century Later." *The Associated Press*, August 11, 1992.

Squire, Louise. "Circles Unrounded: Sustainability, Subject and Necessity in Yann Martel's *Life of Pi*." In *Literature and Sustainability: Concept, Text and Culture*, edited by Adeline Johns-Putra, John Parham, and Louise Squire, 228–45. Manchester: Manchester University Press, 2017.

Stark, Hannah. "'All These Things He Saw and Did Not See': Witnessing the End of the World in Cormac McCarthy's *The Road*." *Critical Survey* 25, no.2 (2013): 71–84.

Stoknes, Per Espen. *What We Think about When We Try Not to Think about Global Warming*. Vermont: Chelsea Green Publishing, 2015.

Sugg, Richard. *Mummies, Cannibals and Vampires: The History of Corpse Medicine from the Renaissance to the Victorians*. 2nd ed. New York: Routledge, 2016.

Suomala, Karla. "Complex Religious Identity in the Context of Interfaith Dialogue." *Crosscurrents: The Association for Religion and Intellectual Life* 62, no. 3 (September 2012): 360–70.

Sutherland, M. A., B. L. Davis, T. A. Brooks, and J. F. Coetzee. "The Physiological and Behavioral Response of Pigs Castrated with and without Anesthesia or Analgesia." *Journal of Animal Science* 90, no. 7 (July 2012): 2211–21.

Tate, Andrew. *Apocalyptic Fiction*. London: Bloomsbury, 2017.

Tedeschi, Richard G., and Lawrence G. Calhoun. "Posttraumatic Growth: Conceptual Foundations and Empirical Evidence." *Psychological Inquiry* 15, no. 1 (2004): 1–18.

Thacker, Eugene. "Notes on Extinction and Existence." *Configurations* 20, nos. 1–2 (Winter–Spring 2012): 137–48.

Trexler, Adam. *Anthropocene Fictions: The Novel in a Time of Climate Change*. Charlottesville: University of Virginia Press, 2015.

Tsing, Anna Lowenhaupt. *The Mushroom at the End of the World: On the Possibility of Life in Capitalist Ruins*. Princeton, NJ: Princeton University Press, 2015.

Turner, Jacqueline A., and Christy G. Turner II. *Man Corn: Cannibalism and Violence in the Prehistoric American Southwest*. Salt Lake City: University of Utah Press, 1999.

United Nations: Food and Agricultural Organization. "Data," n.d. fao.org/faostat/en/#data.

United Nations: Intergovernmental Science-Policy Platform on Biodiversity and Ecosystem Services (IPBES). "UN Report: Nature's Dangerous Decline 'Unprecedented'; Species Extinction Rates 'Accelerating'." May 6, 2019. https://www.un.org/sustainabledevelopment/blog/2019/05/nature-decline-unprecedented-report/.

Vermeulen, Pieter. "Beauty That Must Die: *Station Eleven*, Climate Change Fiction, and the Life of Form." *Studies in the Novel* 50, no. 1 (Spring 2018): 9–25.

Vollhardt, Johanna R. "Altruism Born of Suffering and Prosocial Behavior Following Adverse Life Events: A Review and Conceptualization." *Social Justice Research* 22, no. 1 (2009): 53–97.

Von Hagens, Gunther. "No Skeletons in the Closet: Facts, Background and Conclusions." *Body Worlds*, November 17, 2003. PDF: bodyworlds.com/Downloads/E_Kirgisien%20AW%20GVH%202.pdf.

Von Hagens, Gunther, and Angelina Whalley. *The Anatomical Exhibition of Real Human Bodies*. Heidelberg: Institute for Plastination, 2004.

Wade-Benzoni, Kimberly A., Leigh Plunkett Tost, Morela Hernandez, and Richard P. Larrick. "It's Only a Matter of Time: Death, Legacies, and Intergenerational Decisions." *Psychological Science* 23, no. 7 (June 12, 2012): 704–9.

Wall, Matthew. "Hi-tech Toilets Save Lives—and Mean Big Business." *BBC News*, May 8, 2016.

Wallace-Wells, David. *The Uninhabitable Earth: Life after Warming*. New York: Tim Duggan Books, 2019.

Ward, Peter D. *The Flooded Earth: Our Future in a World Without Ice Caps*. New York: Basic Books, 2010.

Watts, Johnathan. "US and Saudi Arabia Blocking Regulation of Geoengineering, Sources Say." *The Guardian*, March 18, 2019.

Weil, Kari. *Thinking Animals: Why Animals Now?* New York: Columbia University Press, 2012.

Weisman, Alan. *The World without Us*. New York: Thomas Dunne Books, 2007.

Westling, Louise. *The Logos of the Living World: Merleau-Ponty, Animals, and Language*. New York: Fordham University Press, 2014.

Wolfe, Cary. "Condors at the End of the World." In *After Extinction*, edited by Richard Grusin, 107–22. Minneapolis: University of Minnesota Press, 2018.

Wood, James. "Getting to the End." *The New Republic*, May 21, 2007: 44–8.

World Health Organization. "Summary." who.int/globalchange/summary/en/index5.html.

Yeh, Michelle. *Modern Chinese Poetry: Theory and Practice Since 1917*. New Haven, CT: Yale University Press, 1991.

Zaki, Jamil. *The War for Kindness: Building Empathy in a Fractured World*. New York: Crown Publishing Group, 2019.

Zaph, Hubert. "Creative Matter and Creative Mind: Cultural Ecology and Literary Creativity." In *Material Ecocriticism*, edited by Serenella Iovino and Serpil Oppermann, 51–66. Bloomington: University of Indiana Press, 2014.

Zaph, Hubert. "Literary Ecology and the Ethics of Texts." *New Literary History* 38, no. 4 (2008): 1–16.

Zaval, Liza, Ezra M. Markowitz, and Elke U. Weber. "How Will I Be Remembered? Conserving the Environment for the Sake of One's Legacy." *Psychological Science* 26, no. 2 (2015): 231–6.

Zibrak, Arielle. "Intolerance, A Survival Guide: Heteronormative Culture Formation in Cormac McCarthy's *The Road.*" *Arizona Quarterly* 63, no. 3 (Autumn 2012): 103–28.

Zimmer, Carl. "Bones Give Peek into the Lives of Neanderthals." *The New York Times*, December 20, 2010.

Žižek, Slavoj. *The Plague of Fantasies*. London: Verso, 1997.

Index